# ...and GOD CRIED
## *The Holocaust Remembered*

### Charles Lawliss

Published by
JG Press, a Trademark of JG Press, Inc.
Distributed by
World Publications, Inc.
455 Somerset Avenue
North Dighton, MA 02764

Produced by JG Press, Inc.
and Wieser & Wieser, Inc.
118 East 25th Street
New York, NY 10010

Design and typography by Noble Desktop Publishers
Edited by Elizabeth Camplese

ISBN 1-57215-036-X

Printed in the United States of America

# A MESSAGE FROM THE PUBLISHER

*...and God Cried* is a journey through a past that will haunt our tomorrows. It is one of the most important works that we will ever publish.

The photographs we have chosen serve as the visual reality of an anguished history that mere words cannot adequately relate.

We extend our sincere appreciation to the United States National Holocaust Memorial Museum and the Simon Wiesenthal Center for their photographic contributions.

The Simon Wiesenthal Center is the largest institution of its kind in North America—an international center for Holocaust remembrance, the defense of human rights and the Jewish people. Ten percent of our personal profits from the sale of *...and God Cried* will be donated to the Simon Wiesenthal Center Library & Archive to help in their never-ending efforts to educate about anti-semitism and the Holocaust.

Gail & Jeffrey Press
JG Press, Inc.

# Foreword

This book relates in pictures and words a truly gruesome story of man's inhumanity to man.

From 1933 to 1945 Nazi Germany developed and carried out a cruel and systematic annihilation of six million Jews, including one-and-one-half million children.

This criminal plan, referred to as "The Final Solution," was the brainchild of Adolf Hitler, Joseph Goebbels, Martin Bohrmann and other members of a once civilized German society of philosophers and scientists, and was carried out by fanatic S.S. troops, special forces and guards loyal to the Nazi ideal of racial purity.

The book begins with the ugly repression of the Jews in the early years of Hitler's Reich, followed by events leading to "Kristallnacht" and thence to the onset of World War II. The holocaust then swung into high gear with the establishment of labor camps and concentration camps, all breeding disease, poverty and starvation. These facilities were explicitly designed for the mass extermination of those deemed unfit to exist alongside the pure Aryan culture of Nazism.

" ...AND GOD CRIED" also relates a history that was not limited to the destruction of the Jews of Europe, for the Holocaust was also a time of true human spirit that personifies man's courage to resist, to help and to often save one another.

It is our hope that this work will serve as a commemoration for those individuals unjustly victimized by the Nazi regime, and an urgent plea to remember just how effectively hatred and prejudice can flourish in a society when left unchecked.

"... beware ..., lest you forget the things that your eyes have beheld and lest you remove them from your heart..., and make them known to your children and your children's children." (Deuteronomy 4:9).

# Photo Credits

*First they came for the socialists, and I did not
speak out—because I was not a socialist.*

*Then they came for the trade-unionists, and I
did not speak out because I was not a trade-unionist.*

*Then they came for the Jews, and I did not
speak out—because I was not a Jew.*

*Then they came for me—and there was no one
left to speak for me.*

Reverend Martin Niemoller

# Chapter 1

*It is our duty to arouse, to whip up, and to incite in our people the instinctive repugnance of the Jews.*

## Adolf Hitler

The Holocaust is the name given to Nazi Germany's deliberate, methodical killing of between five and six million Jews, nearly 60 percent of Europe's prewar Jewish population. In its magnitude and systematic nature, the Holocaust was an event without parallel. Winston Churchill wrote: "There is no doubt that this is probably the greatest and most horrible crime ever committed in the whole history of the world."

Adolf Hitler's crimes against humanity extended beyond the Holocaust. Gas chambers and execution squads, as well as maltreatment and neglect, claimed the lives of more than 10 million non-Jews who fell into Nazi hands during World War II. This figure includes the often forgotten six million Poles and the millions of Slavs in the Soviet Union who were killed by the Third Reich.

Among Hitler's victims were Catholic priests, Jehovah's Witnesses, Gypsies, Marxists, homosexuals, people with mental and physical handicaps, and anyone considered a political enemy of the Third Reich. In addition to these civilians, more than three million Slavs serving in the Red Army, were taken prisoner of war by the Germans and are believed to have died in their captivity.

These slaughters, conducted far from the combat zone, were, in large measure, the result of the racism that lay at the heart of Nazi ideology. Hitler's doctrine of German racial superiority allowed him to dictate the eradication of those peoples he considered undesirable—above all, the Jews. It gave him license to expand the Reich eastward to obtain *Lebensraum*, or living space, for his master race at the expense of those who lived in the path of conquest.

The fury which drove Adolf Hitler's Final Solution burned with such all-consuming passion that the name *Holocaust* was given to it. In the original Greek, the word "holocaust" described a sacrifice wholly consumed by fire. Implicit in the word is the image of the crematoria in the death camps, the

*Storm troopers block the entrance to a Jewish-owned shop. The signs demand that Germans buy only at German-owned shops. The Star of David was painted in yellow and black across thousands of doors and windows. When the boycott began, German police were told not to hinder it in any way, but rather to "view the boycott with magnanimity." Some Germans made it a point of honor to patronize Jewish shops, others saw the boycott as a sign of things to come. Some Jews fled Germany, most stayed in the hope that the German sense of justice would prevail.*

ovens where the bodies of millions were destroyed. The spark that ignited the Holocaust began in ancient times and smoldered for centuries.

In their ancient beginnings, the Jews were a pastoral people based in the Fertile Crescent. They later settled in Palestine where the Jews established their own legal and religious codes based primarily on the concepts of ethical monotheism and justice as the foundation of all human conduct. They denounced the idolatry, immorality and social injustices of their neighbors, thus making powerful enemies. In this manner, the spark of anti-Semitism was ignited.

Exiled from their homeland, Palestine, during the First century A.D., and under the spreading domain of Christianity, the Jews were scattered and dispersed throughout the known world. Anti-Semitism was sanctioned politically, socially and religiously until it became like a birthright—handed down from one generation to another. During the Middle Ages in particular, Jews were segregated in ghettos, forcibly expelled from their adoptive countries, and murdered individually or *en masse* in organized massacres known as pogroms. There was no one to speak for the Jews.

Inflamed rhetoric and propaganda gripped even Martin Luther, the German theologian who broke with Catholicism and led the Protestant Reformation in the 16th century. He reviled the Jews as "a plague, a pestilence, a pure misfortune for our country." He called them the "thirsty bloodhounds and murderers of all Christendom" and urged his followers to burn their homes and synagogues.

Over the centuries anti-Semitism evolved from a simple religious issue into a complex racial issue. Jews were "a distinct race," it was believed, and their behavior was the result of immutable genetic characteristics. During the 19th century, in the newly formed German Empire, writers seized on these racial theories to feed the rising fever of nationalism. They drew a further conclusion: Jews were an inferior race; Germans a superior one. The word Aryan, which Germans applied to themselves, originally denoted the Indo-European group of languages. The word Semitic referred to the language group that included Hebrew and Arabic.

Among the writers who preached anti-Semitism was Houston Stewart Chamberlain, the son of a British admiral and a German mother. He gained instant acceptance in Germany by marrying the daughter of the revered composer Richard Wagner. In his book *The Foundations of the Nineteenth Century*, Chamberlain wrote that "the degenerate Jew could be distinguished from the master race of Aryans simply by the length of the skull." The book became an immediate bestseller when it was published in 1899. Kaiser Wilhelm II praised it, saying it brought "order to confusion, light to darkness, and proof of what we suspected."

The German nationalist mystique of the Volk lent itself to anti-Semitism. The word *Volk* means "people," but such late 18th-century writers as Gottfried von Herder gave it a metaphysical meaning. As it came to be finally defined, the German *Volk* was an eternal system of values, an unchanging spiritual ideal rooted in the agrarian way of life. The nostalgic ways of the past became linked with the idea of the Aryan race. The Jews came to stand for all that the race abhorred—liberalism, urbanism and modernism itself.

None of this deterred Jews from wanting to live in Germany. The Constitution of 1871 gave them full legal equality. When that occurred, a Jewish member of the Prussian lower house said that "finally, after years of waiting in

Parole der Woche Nr. 27/1942 / Zentralverlag der NSDAP., München　　　0155

*"Whoever wears this symbol is an enemy of our Volk," proclaims this early Nazi poster. German law required all Jews to wear a yellow Star of David sewn to the clothing. From the beginning it was Nazi policy to identify Jews and separate them from the mainstream of German society. The government pursued its racial goals in a highly disciplined manner. Beginning in 1934, Jews and other "ethnic foreigners" were cataloged by the government. In the 1939 census, Jews were listed separately and the list was later used for compiling deportation lists. Most of the men, women and children on the list did not survive World War II.*

vain, we have landed in a safe harbor." And to thousands of Jews fleeing the pogroms of eastern Europe at the turn of the century, Germany did offer a seeming haven.

German Jews, flourishing in business, science and the professions now open to them for the first time, became the most assimilated Jews in Europe. During World War I, over 100,000 of the nation's 540,000 Jews served in the Kaiser's army; 12,000 died. But in postwar defeat, the idea of Germany as a safe harbor for Jews slowly began to crumble. Still, the situation in Germany was better than in other parts of Europe.

In the two years immediately after the First World War, more than 85,000 Jews were murdered in the western Ukraine. In a single town, Proskurov, 1,500 Jews were killed, more than in the previous forty years of pogroms throughout Tsarist Russia. In eastern Poland, in 1918 and 1919, more than 500 Jews were killed in Galicia.

Further killings took place in Hungary, with the overthrow in 1919 of the Communist regime, in which some Jews had played a prominent part. In Berlin, in 1922, anti-Semites murdered Walter Rathenau, the German Foreign Minister, a Jew, and Jewish homes in the city were attacked the following year.

In Rumania, in 1922, Jewish university students were attacked. At Piatra three years later, synagogues and schools were looted and the Jewish cemetery was desecrated. In 1926 a Jewish student was murdered at Czernowitz, and his murderer acquitted. During anti-Jewish riots in Oradea, four synagogues were wrecked. Prayer houses were plundered in Jassy, Targu Ocna and Cluj.

At the same time, anti-Semitism grew alarmingly in Germany. Between 1922 and 1933, there were more than 200 instances in Nuremberg alone of the desecration of Jewish graves. During 1923, the first issue of the anti-Semitic newspaper *Der Stürmer* appeared in Nuremberg; its banner slogan proclaiming "The Jews Are Our Misfortune."

In this Germany of post-war humiliation and the chaotic fervor of fragmented nationalism, Adolf Hitler began his rise to prominence as the self-proclaimed destroyer of the Jewish dream of acceptance in Germany. Born in 1889, he had come of age in Vienna when racial hatred infected the radical political fringes of his native Austria as well as Germany. Anti-Semitic by conviction, Hitler pragmatically perceived the need for an all-purpose enemy to provide a focus for his political struggle. His reading of the history of revolutions, he told a journalist in 1922, had taught him to find a "lightning rod that could conduct and channel the odium of the general masses."

The age-old target, the Jew, became Hitler's lightning rod, and hatred of the Jew was the incandescent center of his National Socialist party's philosophy. Hitler and his Nazis loudly blamed the Jews for every trouble that afflicted Germany—defeat in the war, the harsh Treaty of Versailles, the problems of the Weimar government, Marxism, runaway inflation, economic depression, political corruption, even modern art.

"Hatred, burning hatred," Hitler wrote in 1921. "That is what we want to pour into the souls of millions of fellow Germans, until the flame of rage ignites in Germany and avenges the corrupters of our nation."

The drive for living space was a related aspect of German racial ideology. It would serve as a foundation for Nazism and mass killing. In the late 19th century, Friedrich Ratzel, a Germanist, declared that *Lebensraum*, "living space," was the state's most vital requirement. By 1927, when Hitler proclaimed Germany's need for *Lebensraum* in his book Mein Kampf, the idea had become caught up with racism. As the master race, Hitler preached, Germans deserved to expand their borders eastward all the way to the Ural Mountains of the Soviet Union. The people who stood in the way—200 million Slavs and a few million Jews—were all racially inferior. "Slavs are a mass of born slaves," said Hitler, who referred to them as *Untermenschen*, or subhumans. To make way for the Aryans, Hitler declared, one-third of the Slavs would be driven further eastward into Asia, one-third would be reduced to slavery, and one third would be exterminated.

But all this would have to await the war and the conquest of the lands to the east. Persecution of the Jews, though, began as soon as Hitler came to power in 1933. More than a half-million Jews lived in Germany then, making up less than one percent of the total population. Hitler's initial intent was to launch an officially sanctioned campaign of terror, economic pressure and legislation intended to isolate Jews as enemies of the people.

In the early days of the Third Reich, the primary instruments of terror were the brown-shirted bullies of the *Sturmabteilung* (SA), the Storm Troopers. From their formation in 1921, they had engaged in random acts of violence against both Jews and political opponents of the Nazis, the Socialists and Communists. In 1931 alone, the SA desecrated fifty synagogues and defiled more than a hundred Jewish cemeteries.

By 1933 the Storm Troopers had become the Nazi Party's private army of more than 400,000, and with Hitler in power, their terrorism escalated. There were so many beatings, murders, lootings of Jewish businesses and humiliations —forcing Jews to disrobe in public—that even Hitler became alarmed. The ensuing social disorder of the Storm Troopers' unbridled acts threatened the support of the traditional power brokers, the industrialists and army generals Hitler needed in his rise toward absolute authority.

Restive Storm Troopers demanded action against the Jews. That fact, coupled with the boycott announced by the American Jewish War Veterans in March 1933, demanded a quick but definite response: Hitler ordered a nation-wide boycott of Jewish-owned business. He appointed a committee of fourteen party leaders headed by Julius Streicher, the most notorious anti-Semite of the early Nazis to oversee the boycott. The boycott began April 1, 1933, and was enforced by the Storm Troopers, who stood with arms linked in front of tens of thousands of Jewish shops, offices and retail businesses. The doors and windows of Jewish enterprises were painted with the six-pointed Star of David in yellow on black and plastered with signs warning customers to stay away from the premises.

*Waiting to be deported to a death camp, a man looks hopelessly through a fence somewhere in Hungary. Trains carrying human cargo from every corner of Nazi-occupied Europe rolled into death camps carefully situated along major rail lines. The Reichsbahn, the German railroad, was one of the largest organizations in the Third Reich. It had 1.4 million workers who kept the system in operation. During the Holocaust, their job was to allocate personnel, obtain freight cars, coordinate train schedules, keep the tracks open, drive locomotives and clean the cars.*

While some Germans chose to shop at their favorite stores that day, most recognized and accepted the government's message that tolerance of Jews was at an end. Many Jews, though, were stunned "that this cultured German nation," as a Zionist leader put it, "would resort to such iniquitous things."

On April 7th, a week after the boycott, Hitler launched his legislative assault on the Jews. Non-Aryans were prohibited from the civil service and the practice of law. The number of Jews admitted to high schools and universities was sharply limited. The Reich Chambers of Culture were established, mandatory guilds for workers in the fields of film, theater, music, the fine arts, and journalism. Jews were not permitted to join.

Between 1933 and 1939, some 400 anti-Jewish laws were enacted by the Reichstag, Hitler's rubber-stamp parliament. Two constitutional laws issued in 1935 were called the Nuremberg Laws, and effectively isolated the Jews legally, politically and socially. One law, the Reich Citizenship Law, restricted citizenship to those of "German or kindred blood," thus stripping the Jews of the few shreds of political rights that remained for German citizens. Another decree, the Law for the Protection of German Blood and Honor, prohibited marriage and extramarital sexual intercourse between Jews and Germans. A Jew was defined as someone of any religious preference who had at least one grandparent who had practiced Judaism.

Vigorous enforcment of the Nuremberg Laws and other anti-Semitic measures was suspended in 1936 as Hitler did not want to jeopardize either Germany's recovery from the Depression or the 1936 Olympic Games, which were scheduled to be held in Berlin. Jews hoped the worst was over, and a few of the more than 75,000 who had fled the country returned.

*A flyer distributed by Nazi sympathizers purports to document President Franklin D. Roosevelt's "Jewish ancestry." The Nazis were masters of propaganda, employing distortion, drama and ritual to proclaim their cause. Leaflets were but a starting point—more startling propaganda achievements were the 1936 Olympic Games in Berlin and the Nuremburg Rallies: elaborate demonstrations of Hitler's world-view and power for all the world to see.*

# ROOSEVELT'S JEWISH ANCESTRY

The chart shown below has come as a shocking revelation to millions of American citizens. It explains things in connection with Roosevelt's Administration which can not otherwise be understood.

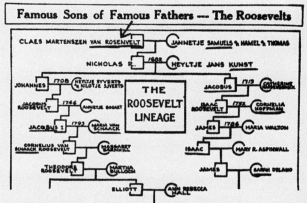

**Famous Sons of Famous Fathers --- The Roosevelts**

(GENEALOGICAL CHART PREPARED IN THE CARNEGIE INSTITUTION OF WASHINGTON, D. C., UNDER DIRECTION OF DR. H. H. LAUGHLIN, PER ASSO. PRESS DISPATCH MAR. 7, 1934, IN THE DAILY CITIZEN OF TUCSON, ARIZ. A SIMILAR CHART WAS PUBLISHED BY THE WASHINGTON, D. C., STAR, OF FEB. 29, 1928)

Even a hasty perusal of this factual document convinces one as to the President's Jewish ancestry. From the viewpoint of eugenics, it explains his natural bent toward radicalism.

It shows why he has given hundreds of so-called Liberals, Socialists and Communists powerful positions in the national government. It reveals the origin of the sinister spirit which today animates the White House. **It proves unmistakably, that the Roosevelt Administration offers a biological, as well as a political problem.**

The New York Times of March 14, 1935, quotes the President as saying: "In the distant past my ancestors may have been Jews. All I know about the origin of the Roosevelt family is that they are apparently descended from Claes Martenszen van Roosevelt, who came from Holland."

Additional information regarding the nationality of the Roosevelt family, was given by Chase S. Osborn, early in 1934, at St. Petersburg, Florida. Mr. Osborn was formerly Governor of Michigan. The leading newspaper of the city (The Times) carried the following report after the interview:

"Although a Republican, the former Governor has a sincere regard for President Roosevelt and his policies. He referred to the 'Jewish ancestry' of the President, explaining how he is a descendant of the Rossocampo family expelled from Spain in 1620. Seeking safety in Germany, Holland and other countries, members of the family, he said, changed their name to Rosenberg, Rosenbaum, Rosenblum, Rosenvelt and Rosenthal.

"The Rosenvelts in north Holland finally became Roosevelt, soon becoming apostates with the first generation and others following suit until, in the fourth generation, a little storekeeper by the name of Jacobus Roosevelt was the only one who remained true to HIS JEWISH FAITH. It is because of this Jewish ancestry, former Governor Osborn said, that President Roosevelt has the trend of economic safety (?) in his veins."

## CONFIRMATION FROM OTHER SOURCES

In the 1938 "World Almanac" under the heading "Biographies of U. S. Presidents and Their Wives," page 237, appears this: "Franklin Delano Roosevelt was the son of James Roosevelt, a direct descendant of Claes Martenzen van ROSENVELT, who arrived in New Amsterdam in 1649 and married Jannetje SAMUELS."

The following is from "The House of Roosevelt" by Paul HABER, 1936 edition "Claes Rosenvelt entered the cloth business in New York, and was married in 1682. He accumulated a fortune. He then changed his name to Nicholas Rosenvelt. Of his four sons, Isaac died young. Nicholas married Sarah Solomons. Jacobus married Catherina Hardenburg. The Roosevelts were not a fighting but a peace-loving people, devoted to trade. Isaac became a capitalist. He founded the Bank of New York in 1790."

The American Freedom Magazine of Los Angeles, Calif., April, 1938, issue, reproduced the quotation below:

"In an address to the National Convention of the D. A. R., President F. D. Roosevelt said that he too was of revolutionary ancestry. BUT NOT A ROOSEVELT WAS IN THE AMERICAN ARMY. They were Tories, busy entertaining British officers. The first Roosevelt came to America in 1649. His name was Claes Rosenfelt. He was a JEW. Nicholas the son of Claes, was the ancestor of both Franklin and Theodore. He married A JEWISH GIRL named Kunst in 1682. Nicholas had a son named Jacobus Rosenfelt. In the family tree there are 351 persons bearing biblical names of the Tribe of Israel —From The Corvallis Gazette-Times, of Corvallis, Oregon."

Roosevelt inevitably draws upon his Semitic ancestry. It is, therefore, as natural for him to be a radical, as it is for others to be true Americans. This is why he can boast of flouting conventionalities, and publicly gloat over destroying those traditions which are fundamental to our national character. HE IS NOT ONE OF US! This may also explain why he attaches so little importance to his word of honor, and has no hesitation in breaking his promises.

In truth, the campaign against the Jews was escalating. Government policy kept public agencies and their employees from patronizing Jewish firms. This policy was incumbent to all Nazi party members and was strictly enforced. The next step was to take businesses away from the Jews. Hermann Göring, Hitler's new economic czar, stepped up the program known as *aryanization*, which permitted the seizure of Jewish enterprises.

New government decrees broadened the definition of Jewish enterprises to include any business "predominately under Jewish influence." This might include a business with a single Jew on the board of directors, or a Jewish legal representative. All Jews with property valued at more than 5,000 marks had to register with the government before November, 1938. *Aryanization* had been voluntary; after, it became compulsory. Other decrees shut down Jewish shops and services, including the professional practices of Jewish physicians.

To understand what was happening in Germany, to understand what lay in store for the Jews, it is necessary to know more about Adolf Hitler, the Austrian corporal, the second-rate painter who, in 1938, was unopposed as Germany's absolute dictator.

# Chapter 2

*Grit your teeth and think revenge.*

## Adolf Hitler

Adolf Hitler was the personal embodiment of Nazi Germany and the evil that flowed from it. For the people of the Allied and conquered countries in World War II, Hitler was the real enemy. He was the strutting, shouting dictator who had to be stopped before he and his diabolic philosophy engulfed the world. Topple Hitler, they believed, and the evil would end.

If this were a simplistic view of a complex war, it is a view confirmed by history. In his biography *Adolf Hitler*, John Toland concludes: "To the surprise of the world, Hitler's death brought an abrupt, absolute end to National Socialism. Without its only true leader, it burst like a bubble. No other leader's death since Napoleon had so completely obliterated a regime."

Adolf Hitler probably was a madman; he certainly was a fanatic. For one thing, he was convinced that he had a vision. It had come to him while being treated for temporary blindness from exposure to mustard gas in the Western Front trenches of World War I. What he envisioned was a command from fate.

In his vision, Hitler was an Aryan hero selected by the ancient Teutonic gods to bestow upon Germany the "Thousand-Year Reich." With the vision came a miracle—the restoration of his sight—and a summons to destiny. At that moment, he would later say, he decided to abandon his art studies and enter politics in order to save Germany.

Germany had a mystic hold on Hitler. He considered it his rightful native land, even though he was born in the Austrian border town of Braunau am Inn in 1889. After the death of his father, when Adolf was thirteen years old, his mother moved the family to Linz, which he would look upon as his real hometown. Later, his first conquest would be Austria, joining it to Germany and uniting the "racial comrades" of the two countries.

Hitler loved his mother and feared his father, whose birth name was Alois Schicklgruber. When Hitler became infamous, Shicklgruber was often used as a comic name for Hitler. The origin of the name was not well known. It was the maiden name of his paternal grandmother who was unmarried when Alois was born. She later married a man named Hiedler. When Alois grew up he took as his name Alois Hitler.

*Joseph Goebbels, Reich Minister for Public Enlightenment and Propaganda, addresses the crowd during the May 10, 1933 book-burning orgy at Berlin's Opernplatz. Thousands of Nazi students and their professors stormed libraries, universities and bookstores in thirty German cities, removed hundreds of thousands of books and cast them onto bonfires. The Nazis were serving notice that they intended to "purify" German culture. Goebbels triumphantly told the crowd: "The age of hairsplitting Jewish intellectualism is dead. The past lies in the flames."*

*In Berlin, on January 31, 1933, Hitler poses with the Nazi leadership. The day before, he had been appointed Germany's Chancellor, an act that sealed the destruction of constitutional government in Germany. A month later, the Reichstag fire would give him the opportunity to consolidate his power. From left to right: Wilhelm Kube, Fritz Sauckel, Wilhelm Frik (seated), Joseph Goebbels, Ernst Roehm, Hermann Göring, Walter Darre, Heinrich Himmler and Rudolf Hess. Curiously, only Himmler is in uniform. After Hitler rose to power, he and the leading Nazis always wore uniforms for public appearances.*

Hitler's beloved mother died in 1907, and in his grief, Hitler led an aimless life in Vienna and Munich, half-heartedly trying to turn his small talent into a career as an artist. When war came in 1914, he scorned service in the Austrian army to volunteer for a Bavarian infantry regiment. As a dispatch runner in the front lines, he was awarded the Iron Cross, First Class, but he was only a corporal when mustard gas ended his military career.

Still aimless but now summoned by destiny, Hitler joined the rebellious veterans and jobless workers who were turning the streets of Munich and Berlin into battlefields. These became the *Freikorps*, private forces fighting the government and each other; some were Communists, some were Socialists, some were Social Democrats , and a few were in the German Worker's Party, which, Hitler, after some soul searching, joined in September,

1919. "I finally came to the conviction that I had to take this step," he wrote. The party later prefixed "National Socialist" to its name, becoming, in German, *Nationalsozialistische Deutsche Arbeiterpartei*, or Nazi for short.

Nazis soon became notorious for their hatred of Jews. They scrawled on the walls and windows of Jewish stores, *Jüde Verrecke!* —Death to Judaism!— using the word reserved for the killing of cattle, *verrecke*. The message was there on the wall, but in the beginning most of the potential victims paid it little attention.

Hitler, with a fanatical belief in his own mission and a gift for enthralling, heart-stirring oratory, rose quickly in the Nazi party and was its leader by 1921. He began making changes. He gave the Nazi party symbols of power. His followers wore brown-shirted uniforms and were called Storm Troopers. Their appearance and conduct inspired fear. He created the Nazi flag, a red banner with a black swastika in a white circle. However, he did not create the swastika. This was an archaic good-luck symbol of many people from the ancient Egyptians to the American Indians. He did propose the Nazi salute of an outstretched arm, accompanied with cries of "Heil Hitler!" or *"Seig Heil!"*— "Hail to victory!"

Hitler appealed to the German people by constantly reminding them of their humiliating defeat in World War I. He repeated the popular myth that the German armies had been "stabbed in the back" by the collapse of the home front. He railed at the wrongs done Germany by the Treaty of Versailles. He damned democracy. He laced all of this with virulent anti-Semitism. He blamed the Jews for all the ills of Germany and of the world, past and present.

When Hitler addressed a crowd he wore the uniform of a Storm Trooper. Surrounded by thousands of uniformed Nazis, he spoke of going to war, a war of revenge against France, Russia, the United States, Wall Street—and the Jews.

"Grit your teeth and think revenge!" he would scream. "Learn how to settle with the men who hurled you into the abyss! We do not want the thing they [the Jews] call unity, which includes everything that is rotten; what we want is struggle; struggle against Jewish democracy, which is no more nor less than a machine for the elimination of genius."

Two years later, he planned a *putsch* —a revolutionary thrust for power— but he badly overestimated both the strength of his frenzied but weak party and his own magnetism. The *putsch* would start November 11, 1923, the fifth anniversary of Germany's surrender. Hitler plotted to seize railroad, telegraph and police stations, take over local governments throughout Bavaria, arrest Communists and labor leaders, and proclaim a provisional government and the start of a new Germany.

The revolution was to be launched from a Munich beer hall, where the commissioner of Bavaria was holding a mass "patriotic demonstration." The party's brown-shirted storm troopers and other armed Nazis surrounded the beer hall. At the appointed moment, Hitler burst in on the meeting, brandishing a pistol, and led an armed group to the speaker's platform. Firing the pistol into the ceiling, he shouted for quiet, and began haranguing the crowd. As the night wore on, amid confusing rhetoric, the Nazi uprising failed to catch fire.

The following morning, under the party's swastika banners, Hitler led 3,000 unruly followers into the center of Munich. Police fired on the mob,. and in the rioting three policemen and sixteen party members were killed. One of the many wounded Nazis was Hermann Göring, who was spirited away from the scene by his wife.

Hitler and nine others were arrested and tried on the charge of high treason. The trial was widely publicized and he was the star. It marked the beginning of his rise to power. He told the court that his accusers were the real traitors. "I feel myself the best of the Germans who wanted the best for the German people," he told the judge. The trial lasted twenty-four days, and on one of them he spoke uninterrupted for four hours. Overnight, the leader of an obscure political party had become a national figure.

Hitler was found guilty and could have been sentenced to life imprisonment. Instead, he was handed a five-year sentence in Landsberg am Lech, a

Prisoners line up for roll call at Buchenwald. All but a few of the new arrivals have had their heads shaved, ostensibly for cleanliness but actually part of a number of measures taken to humiliate them. The Gestapo was authorized to hold people in "protective custody," a euphemism for arbitrary arrest and imprisonment in camps such as Buchenwald. In the first days of the Nazi regime, thousands of political prisoners were arrested and placed in camps. Dachau, established in 1933, was the model for the camps and a training ground for camp personnel. Buchenwald was established in 1937. It was here at Buchenwald that Ilse Koch, the wife of the commandant, amused herself by having lampshades made from the skins of tattooed executed prisoners.

Bavarian prison known for its lenient policies (visitation hours were virtually unlimited, and prisoners could purchase beer and wine for moderate prices). He served only nine months of his sentence, spending his time writing and polishing his rhetoric. A prison guard recalled: "Before we saw the last of him, everyone here, from the governor to the furnace man, had become a convinced believer in his ideas."

In his cell, Hitler wrote his autobiography. Rudolf Hess, a devoted disciple, gave him editorial and secretarial help. Hitler wanted to title his book, "Four-and-a-Half Years of Struggle Against Lies, Stupidity and Cowardice," but a publisher suggested it might sell better if the title were *Mein Kampf* ("My Struggle").

As the Munich putsch became the revered myth of Nazi martyrdom, *Mein Kampf* became the Nazi testament. In later years, each new SS regiment would carry an eagle-topped standard dedicated by Hitler, who touched it with the "Blood Flag" borne by those who fell at Munich in 1923. When Hitler ultimately gained power, every household in Germany had to have a copy of *Mein Kampf*. By reading Hitler's book, one knew what to expect from him and the Nazis.

A great portion of *Mein Kampf* 's rhetoric focused on anti-Semitism: "He [the Jew] stops at nothing, and in his vileness he becomes so gigantic that no one need be surprised if among our people the personification of the devil as the symbol of all evil assumes the living shape of the Jew . . .

"I understood the infamous spiritual terror which this movement exerts, particularly on the bourgeoisie, which is neither morally nor mentally equal to such attacks . . . I achieved an equal understanding of the importance of physical terror toward the masses . . .

"The power which has always started the greatest religious and political avalanches in history rolling has from time immemorial been the magic power of the spoken word, and that alone . . .

"A majority can never replace the man . . . Just as a hundred fools do not make one wise man, a heroic decision is not likely to come from a hundred cowards."

As a religious underpinning for Nazism, Hitler cooked up a strange mixture of Christianity and Teutonic paganism. "I am now convinced," he wrote in *Mein Kampf*, "that I am acting as an agent of our Creator by fighting off the Jews. I am doing the Lord's work."

Hitler even attempted to explain why Jesus was not a Jew. Twisting Catholic dogma, Hitler held that Jesus' mother, Mary, was conceived without physical intercourse. And, since Jesus' father was God, Jesus was therefore not Jewish through either of his parents. He could not get around the fact that

Mary's parents had to be Jewish. Under Nazi doctrine, that made Jesus a *Mischling*, a nonpracticing half-Jew.

To his perversion of Christianity, Hitler linked a mystical belief in the Teutonic gods and goddesses of the operas of Richard Wagner, also an anti-Semite. From Wagner's *Parsifal*, for example, Hitler said he had learned that "you can serve God only as a hero." He revered Wagner, and made frequent visits to the composer's family, leading romantic Germans to expect that he would marry Winifred Wagner, widow of Wagner's son Siegfried.

Out of prison, Hitler rebuilt his Nazi party, and at Party Day in Weimar in 1926, and again at Nuremberg in 1927, many speakers advocated driving the Jews out of German life. In 1927, Jewish cemeteries were desecrated by Nazi gangs, and synagogues were wrecked at Osnabruck and Krefeld. In Berlin in 1931, the eve of the Jewish New Year, Nazis attacked Jews returning from synagogue.

Privately, Hitler led a life of austerity. He was a vegetarian who neither smoked nor drank. He was a bachelor. When a newly married secretary jokingly reminded him that he urged marriage on everyone but himself, he said that he did not want to be a father. He added that "the children of a genius have a hard time in this world. One expects such a child to be a replica of his famous father and doesn't forgive him for being average."

He did seem to have an eye for pretty girls. There was speculation about his relationship with his niece Geli Raubal, nineteen years his junior. He was frequently seen with her, and seemed proud to show off her blonde beauty. The romance ended tragically in 1931, when, after quarrels that seemed to be triggered by Hitler's jealousy, Geli killed herself with a pistol. The suicide occurred in Hitler's large Munich apartment where Geli lived with her sister and her mother, Hitler's half-sister who served as his housekeeper. Two years before the tragic incident, Hitler had met Eva Braun, a seventeen-year-old Munich shop girl.

Hitler's rise to power was not meteoric. In 1928, after five years of rebuilding the party and trying to achieve power by constitutional means, the Nazi party received only 810,000 votes out of 31 million cast in the national elections, and Hitler was a political joke.

Then came the economic collapse of 1929. As unemployment rose, the Nazis skillfully exploited the growing despair. In 1930, the Nazis got more than six million votes to become the second largest party in Germany. In 1932, they gained nearly fourteen million votes, which made them the largest.

The German Communist Party also had grown with hard times, but Hitler proved more adept at intrigue. He carefully cultivated political alliances with the army generals, the industrialists, and with the nationalist politicians. The president of the German Federal Republic was the eighty-six-year-old Paul von Hindenburg, a field marshal in the First World War. In the election of 1932, the aristocratic Hindenburg was reelected, defeating Hitler whom he casually dismissed as "the Bohemian corporal."

As Hitler rose to power, however, Hindenburg had to deal with him, and decided to bring him into the government. As Hitler gained political power, he only seemed to become more temperate. "He has stopped breathing fire at the Jews and can make a speech nowadays lasting for four hours without mentioning the word 'Jew'," remarked Hindenberg as he prepared to elevate Hitler to the office of Chancellor of Germany.

# Chapter 3

*Where one burns books, one will,
in the end, burn people.*

**Heinrich Heine**

On January 30, 1933, Adolf Hitler was named Chancellor of Germany, and became the head of a coalition government of his National Socialists and the right-wing Nationalist party. Hindenburg and his advisors hoped that Hitler could end the political chaos and still be restrained. Apparently no one in high office was listening when Joseph Goebbels, the Nazi master propagandist, made clear what Germany should expect: "We come like wolves descending upon a herd of sheep."

The Weimar Constitution, under which Germany was governed, contained a fatal flaw. Emergency provisions allowed the president to usurp the constitutional powers of the state governments, suspend the constitutional guarantees of civil liberties and dissolve the Reichstag. The Reichstag could also grant temporary legislative power to the Chancellor. Here were the openings Hitler needed to seize power.

Less than a month after Hitler became Chancellor on February 27, the Reichstag building was set afire. Hitler blamed the Communists and persuaded Hindenburg to invoke the emergency powers. Four thousand Communists were arrested, as well as Social Democrats, liberal leaders and members of the Reichstag. A "shoot-to-kill" order encouraged police to fire on demonstrators. In the last few days before the March election, Storm Troopers created violent disturbances throughout the country. From the chaos, the Nazis won 44 percent of the popular vote.

The Reichstag reconvened and gave Hitler dictatorial powers. As a result, the Weimar Republic was effectively dead; the Reichstag little more than a rubber stamp. For the next twelve years, Germany would be ruled by the *Führer*.

Hitler moved swiftly to gather all state power into his hands, and carry out the Nazification of German culture. On April 7, the governments of the

German federal states were dissolved and Nazi governors appointed. May 1 was declared a workers' holiday, and labor leaders were invited to participate in parades and celebrations. The next day, trade-union leaders were arrested; within the month, all labor unions had ceased to exist.

The judiciary was also brought under tight Nazi control. By early May, a People's Court was established to try treason cases. Proceedings were secret,

*Nazi storm troopers pass out propaganda literature in Berlin during the boycott of Jewish businesses and shops throughout Germany, which began on April 1, 1933. The boycott was Hitler's response to foreign criticism of his regime. Reports of Nazi violence against Jews and Jewish businesses in Germany had prompted talk of an American boycott of German goods. Hitler struck first. On March 26, he told Joseph Goebbels: "We must proceed to a large-scale boycott of Jewish businesses in Germany. Perhaps the foreign Jews will think better of the matter when their racial comrades in Germany begin to get it in the neck."*

and there was no way to appeal a verdict except to Hitler. Death sentences were handed down routinely. Between May and July, all opposing political parties were dissolved. On July 14, 1933, the National Socialist party was declared the sole party in Germany.

That same day, the Law for the Prevention of Hereditary and Defective Offspring was proclaimed. This law authorized the surgical sterilization of people who were mentally retarded, schizophrenic, alcoholic or genetically diseased.

Hitler soon had formed an all-Nazi government dedicated to his racial beliefs. In addition to the normal government agencies that controlled such functions as transportation, agriculture and banking, agencies were created to control the German people. One of Hitler's goals was to make Germany *judenrein*, free of Jews. He first intended to make Jews leave the country voluntarily.

Hermann Göring, Hitler's second-in-command, ran the Gestapo, the dreaded secret police. The Gestapo had a power above that of the courts. If a court found a defendant not guilty, the Gestapo still could arrest and imprison the individual. Joseph Goebbels, in charge of propaganda, controlled all media—newspapers, magazines, movies, radio stations and theaters.

The SS, Hitler's elite black-shirted personal guard, became a political force that symbolized Nazi terrorism and slaughter. The *Schutzstaffel* ("protection detachment," abbreviated as SS) started as a tiny, highly disciplined unit with only 280 members. It began to grow after Hitler placed Heinrich Himmler in charge. By 1930, he had recruited more than 3,000 members, each a paragon of racial purity. The SS motto was *"Meine Ehre heisst Treue"* ("Loyalty is My Honor.") Waffen (military) SS divisions would fight alongside the Wehrmacht (army) but were answerable only to Hitler. The SS also ran the concentration camps. These troops wore the *Totenkopfverbände* or Death's-Head insignia.

SS duties often overlapped those of the Gestapo. The SS conducted door-to-door searches, and had its own intelligence unit, the *Sicherheitsdienst*, or SD, whose duty, according to Himmler, was to "discover the enemies of the National Socialist concept." Reinhard Heydrich was in charge of the SD. He would soon play an important role in Hitler's plan for the Jews, as would Adolf Eichmann, whom Heydrich appointed to head a department of Jewish affairs.

The Nazi party continued to function as a political party. It had branches in every neighborhood and searched for people who were not loyal to Hitler. It organized school children into Hitler Youth groups, in which they wore swastika armbands and were taught to hate Jews. Children were encouraged to spy on their parents and report anyone who said anything against Hitler or the party.

Throughout Germany, the press regularly printed false reports of Jewish treachery, such as stories about Jews drinking the blood of a Christian child, and other lies. Movie theaters, concert halls, cafes and other public places put up signs reading "Jews Not Wanted." Signs at swimming pools read "No Jews or Dogs." Cabaret entertainers ridiculed Jews. One staged a mock wedding between a German and a pig, which wore a sign that said that it was a Jew.

Hatred and suspicion were everywhere. Jews were shunned by their neighbors, and former friends would not greet them in the street. Police looked the other way when Jews were attacked and Jewish homes and stores were looted. School children felt free to bully their Jewish classmates.

On the night of May 10, 1933, thousands of Nazi students stormed universities, libraries and bookstores in thirty German cities, removed hundreds of thousands of books and threw them onto bonfires. The book burnings were part of a calculated effort to "purify" German culture. For nearly a month, the Nazi German Student Association had been purging libraries, working from lists of books considered "un-German."

The book burnings were designed as a spectacle with torchlight parades, frenzied dancing, ritualistic chants, and the massive bonfires. At one book burning, held opposite the main entrance to the University of Berlin, Joseph Goebbels told a cheering crowd: "The age of hairsplitting Jewish intellectualism is dead . . . The past lies in the flames."

Among the Jewish authors whose books were burned were Albert Einstein, Sigmund Freud and Stefan Zweig. The works of Nobel Prize winner Thomas Mann, Germany's best-known author, were cast into the flames. Other eminent German-language writers whose books were burned were Bertolt Brecht, Franz Werfel and Erich Maria Remarque. American authors were not spared. In the flames were books by Jack London, Ernest Hemingway, Upton Sinclair, John Dos Passos, Theodore Dreiser and Sinclair Lewis. Walter Lippmann, the political commentator, perceptively wrote: "There is a government in Germany which means to teach its people that their salvation lies in violence."

On April 1, 1933, Hitler launched a boycott of Jewish businesses, saying, "I believe that I act today in unison with the Almighty Creator's intention: by fighting the Jews I do battle for the Lord." The boycott was enforced by Storm Troopers who stood at the entrances to Jewish shops and stores, intimidating anyone who dared to enter. Signs were posted saying: "Germans! Defend Yourselves! Don't Buy From Jews" or simply "*Jüde.*"

Goebbels was driven around Berlin to see how the boycott was progressing and noted in his diary: "All Jews' businesses are closed. SA men are posted outside their entrances. The public has everywhere proclaimed its

*Reinhard Heydrich, called the "Blond Beast," was the Chief of the Reich Central Security Office and one of the principal planners of Germany's Final Solution for the Jews. In the 1930s Heydrich, who had been forced to resign from the German Navy in 1931 for "conduct unbecoming to an officer and a gentleman" after seducing a young girl, became a close associate of Heinrich Himmler and was given command of the Gestapo. By 1936, the Gestapo seemed to be everywhere. Block wardens monitored their neighbors, waiters informed on their patrons, workers were alert to disparaging comments about the Nazi regime by their employers. Children were taught to watch their teachers, their pastors, even their parents. The Gestapo's reputation for cruelty only made it more feared, respected and effective. When the war began, Heydrich launched Operation Reinhard, the plan for the systematic extermination of the Jews of Poland. On May 27, 1942, two Czech agents ambushed Heydrich's car and fatally wounded him. In an orgy of bloody reprisals, SS men razed the Czech village of Lidice and killed all its inhabitants. More than 1,000 Czechs elsewhere were sentenced to death, and 3,000 inmates of the Theresienstadt camp for Jews were sent to the gas chambers.*

solidarity. The discipline is exemplary. An imposing performance! . . . There is indescribable excitement in the air."

A week later, Hitler removed Jews from the civil service. Before the year was out "non-Aryans"—Jews or anyone who had one Jewish parent or grandparent—were removed from the legal and medical professions, journalism, banks and the stock exchange.

In September 1933, the Nazi party held its first annual rally at Nuremberg. Party members, from Hitler down to the village block leader, regenerated their enthusiasm and faith in a week-long delirium of parades, speeches, music and pagan pageantry.

Nothing was spared to make the rally a memorable experience. Torchlight parades and other night spectacles were frequent. Hitler believed that "in the evening the people's willpower more easily succumbs to the dominating force of a stronger will." The finale was a speech by Hitler that sent both him and

the thousands in his audience into emotional frenzies. An American observer, reporter and author William L. Shirer, said, "They looked up at him as if he were a Messiah."

In the fall of 1935, the Nazis pushed through the Reichstag the Nuremberg Laws. A "blood" law stipulated that only persons of "German or related blood" could be citizens. Jews became *staatsangehörige*, subjects who belong to the state. "The Law for the Protection of German Blood and German Honor" prohibited marriage or sexual relations between Jews and non-Jews.

Regulations stemming from these laws led to the withdrawal of political rights and to outright persecution of the Jews. Using the pretext of Nuremberg law violations, Nazis seized Jewish business and authorized the breaking of commercial contracts and the dismissal of Jewish employees. Eventually, Jewish children were barred from attending public schools.

At first, the Jews could not comprehend what was happening to them. Jews had lived on German soil since the time of the Roman Empire. Despite often savage persecution in medieval times, and frequent expulsions from town to town, they had continued over a period of sixteen centuries, to make important contributions to the development of modern Germany.

In the Weimar Republic, Jews had served in high office, held important civil service positions, taught in the great universities. Their influence in German intellectual life was great. Of the thirty-eight Nobel Prizes won by Germans between 1905 and 1936, fourteen were awarded to Jews.

Until Hitler came to power, Germany had represented culture and freedom to the European Jewish community. Jews were active in the arts, science and literature, industry and the professions. True, there was social discrimination and Jews were often limited in their careers, but they were as comfortable as Germans. Many converted to Christianity, and even more abandoned their traditional religious practices. Intermarriage between Christians and Jews was common.

Jews believed they had demonstrated their loyalty to Germany during the First World War. More than 100,000, one in every six Jews in the population, had served in the Kaiser's army, 80 percent of them in combat roles. Twelve thousand had been killed in the war; thirty-five thousand had been decorated for bravery.

The German-Jewish newspaper *Jüdische Rundschau* could read the handwriting on the wall. It gave its readers a carefully worded warning: "We live in a new period, the national revolution of the German people is a signal that indicates that the world of our previous concepts has collapsed . . . . The only survivors will be those who are able to look reality in the eye."

Jews who looked reality in the eye began to leave Germany. Those who could afford it went to America and other countries far out of Hitler's reach. A Jewish welfare agency, the American Joint Distribution Committee, helped others get to Palestine. The remainder couldn't believe that the madness would continue.

Between 1933 and 1938, the first concentration camps opened: Dachau, near Munich; Sachsenhausen, near Kassel; and Buchenwald, near Weimar, the capital of the democracy the Nazis destroyed. Within a year, there would be fifty camps located all over Germany. Practices were developed that would become standard in the hundreds of camps that sprang up during the war. On arrival, prisoners had their heads shaved and identification numbers tattooed on their forearms. They were given tunics and pants of cheap, striped cloth. Like everything in the camps, these measures were designed to dehumanize the inmates.

Critics of the regime were sent to these camps, as were thousands of individuals against whom Nazi hatred was directed, including homosexuals (for whom the law was particularly severe), socialists, communists, dissident

Hitler's head of propaganda, Joseph Goebbels, addresses a Berlin rally supporting the boycott of Jewish businesses and stores throughout Germany. The boycott marked the beginning of official persecution of the Jews in Germany. Signs were posted saying: "Don't Buy from Jews," "The Jews Are Our Misfortune," or simply "Jude."

clergymen as well as Jews. By July 1933, 26,789 people were in "protective custody" in the camps. Prisoners were forced to perform back-breaking labor for fourteen to sixteen hours a day. Those who complained or lagged behind were tied to trees and beaten. Brutality by guards led to many deaths from the first days of Hitler's rule. By 1935, at least forty-five Jews had been murdered at Dachau alone.

At Buchenwald, Ilse Koch, the wife of a sadistic SS colonel, participated in the killing of hundreds of prisoners. She also had the perverse hobby of collecting lamp shades, book covers and gloves made from the skin of dead prisoners. Camp guards were under orders to notify her of new prisoners having interesting tattoos. If Frau Koch approved, the prisoners would be killed by lethal injection, the tatooed skin carefully removed by the pathology department and turned over to her to be made into artifacts. She soon became known as "The Bitch of Buchenwald."

In July, 1935, the English newspaper *Manchester Guardian* published a description of the Gestapo interrogating a prisoner: "His head was wrapped in a wet cloth that was knotted so tightly across his mouth that his teeth cut into his lips and his mouth bled profusely. He was held by three assistants while the official and another assistant took turns in beating him with a flexible leather-covered steel rod. When he fainted from pain and loss of blood he was brought to by means of various other tortures . . . He was told that he might write a letter to his wife, as he would never see her again. The assistants fingered their pistols and discussed which of them should shoot the prisoner. But he remained silent. He was released sometime afterwards."

As an alternative to the stick, Hitler offered the carrot of propaganda. In *Mein Kampf* he wrote that propaganda, to be successful, had to present a simple message to a mass audience. The German people had to believe they were involved in an urgent struggle with an evil enemy. He placed Dr. Joseph Goebbels in charge of the Ministry of Public Enlightenment and Propaganda to control the flow of public information through the media.

All newspapers were licensed, and those who did not follow the Nazi party line were shut down. Some of the most venerable newspapers were either closed because they were owned by Jews, or were forced to get rid of their Jewish employees. Goebbels held daily press briefings to instruct the press which events would be covered and how. Failure to please him by printing anything "to weaken the strength of the German Reich . . . or offend the honor and dignity of Germany" could result in heavy fines or imprisonment in a concentration camp.

The state-owned broadcasting system was turned into a propaganda vehicle. A cheap wireless radio called the *Volksempfänger* was marketed, and local radio wardens encouraged neighbors to buy them. People could be arrested for listening to foreign broadcasts. Radio reached a mass audience and became the most pervasive source of Nazi propaganda.

The theme of all Nazi propaganda was the cult of the *Führer,* the great charismatic leader. It was designed to shape a folk community bonded to its leader. Allegiance to Hitler was direct, personal and absolute, transcending and superseding all other loyalties.

Germans were constantly told they were racially superior. Slavs, Gypsies and blacks were inferior; Jews were the worst of all, in part because they parasitically lived off the other races and weakened them. The Aryan race was destined to be superior, which meant the German people "are the highest species of humanity on earth." But this master race would prevail only if it preserved its purity. Otherwise, the master race would be polluted, corrupted and destroyed by inferior races.

Sometimes Nazi propaganda could be sophisticated. Hitler's frequent companion, Leni Riefenstahl, a beautiful film star and director, glorified the *Führer* in *Triumph of the Will*, a ninety-minute film of the 1934 Nazi party rally at Nuremberg. The film is a masterpiece of elegant technique.

And sometimes the propaganda could be crude. *Der Stürmer*, a popular tabloid published by Julius Streicher, featured crude anti-Semitic cartoons and childish stories in which Jews were engaged in international conspiracies, or businessmen cheating honest Germans, or sex-crazed monsters violating German women.

The most impressive achievement of Dr. Goebbels' propaganda was the public relations effort that surrounded the 1936 Olympics in Berlin. The Nazis wanted to show the world the new Germany that had risen from the ashes of World War I. They also wanted to convince the international community that they had been unfairly treated by the press.

Many Americans opposed participation in the Olympics in the belief that it would be taken as a tacit approval of the Nazi regime. The American Olympic Committee decided to go ahead after it was given false assurances about the participation of Jewish athletes. Before the games began, Berlin was cleaned up. Anti-Semitic posters and billboards were removed. Nazi rhetoric was toned down.

Hitler was very much in evidence at the games. His arrivals and departures were dramatically staged, and he personally congratulated the German medalists. Hopes for an Aryan triumph were spoiled when Jesse Owens, a black American, won an unprecedented four gold medals. On the other hand, Avrey Brundage, president of the American Olympic Committee, withdrew two U.S. Jewish runners from the finals of the 400-meter relay because he was afraid a victory by Jewish athletes would further offend the German hosts.

Dignitaries returning from Berlin reassured President Roosevelt, who had been silent throughout the Olympic debate. Said one, "The synagogues were crowded and apparently there is nothing very wrong."

# Chapter 4

*How horrible, fantastic, incredible it is that we should be digging trenches and trying on gas masks here because of a quarrel in a faraway country between people of whom we know nothing.*

## Neville Chamberlain

In October, 1933, Hitler took Germany out of the League of Nations and the Geneva Disarmament Conference, claiming that his country was not given equality with other nations. This act made it clear that Germany would rearm in defiance of the Treaty of Versailles. The Allies did nothing. Hitler had correctly judged the mettle of his adversaries.

In March 1935, Hitler revealed the existence of a German air force and a program to build a peacetime army of thirty-six divisions. The Allies protested but again did nothing. In 1936, Hitler sent troops into the demilitarized Rhineland in direct violation of the Treaty of Versailles. His generals had advised against the move, certain it would bring a French retaliation, but again Hitler had correctly predicted the timidity of the democracies. The last chance to stop Hitler, short of war, now was lost.

With an efficient war machine and his border secure, Hitler turned to expanding the Third Reich. His first victim was Austria. On March 11, 1938, German troops occupied Austria, receiving a warm welcome from the population. Two days later, *Anschluss*, the union of Austria with Germany. was announced by Hitler.

For Austrian Jews, *Anschluss* meant disaster. In a year, the Nazis totally excluded the Jews, setting a pattern to be followed in other occupied lands. Austria had a long tradition of anti-Semitism, and many Austrian politicians set out to prove that they disliked Jews as much as the Nazis did.

When the Germans came, there were 185,000 Jews in Austria, most of them living in Vienna. Suddenly Jews were being attacked on the streets. The beards of Orthodox Jews were forcibly shaved. While crowds jeered, Jewish women were compelled to scrub streets. Order of a sort was restored, but anti-Semitism continued in more sinister forms.

The SS established the Central Office for Jewish Emigration under the direction of Adolf Eichmann—the German-born, Austrian-raised "Jewish specialist." It was housed in a mansion confiscated from Baron Louis de Rothchild. A concentration camp was built at the town of Mauthausen so that Austrians taken into "protective custody" would not have to be shipped to Germany.

By the summer of 1939, over 27,000 Jewish businesses were closed, 5,000 of them transferred to non-Jewish ownership. Sixty percent of all Jewish apartments and homes were taken over for Aryan use. Jews began leaving Austria; by September, nearly three out of four were gone.

Two weeks after the *Anschluss*, Hitler was already planning his strategy against Czechoslovakia, the most prosperous and most democratic country in central Europe. First he insisted on protecting the Sudeten German minority, then he demanded the annexation of the Sudetenland. Certain that the Allies would go to war over Czechoslovakia, the German General Staff cautioned Hitler that his army was not prepared.

Hitler, however, was convinced that the major Allied supporters of Czechoslovakia would capitulate in order not to risk war with Germany. Both France and Britain, who had treaty obligations to support Czechoslovakia, in Munich agreed to Hitler's annexation of the Sudetenland. Thus, in September 1938, the Allies left Munich, naively believing the sacrifice of the Sudetenland insured a larger European peace.

Without the Sudetenland, Czechoslovakia was defenseless and bankrupt. The region had contained her fortifications and most of her mines and industry. Hitler ignored his pledge to respect the newly imposed Czech borders and began a systematic campaign which ended with German troops occupying the entire country. Thus, on March 15, 1939, Czech Nazis cheered when Adolf Hitler himself entered Prague to announce Czechoslovakia's annexation to Germany.

In England the national outcry forced Prime Minister Chamberlain to censure Hitler in the House of Commons for the rape of Czechoslovakia and declare a firmer position against Hitler's aggression. France and England agreed to defend the integrity of Poland against any outside threat, as it was obvious that Poland would be Hitler's next acquisition.

Although Britain and France asked Russia to join with them to stop German aggression, Stalin refused and subsequently cast his lot with Hitler. Angry at the way his leadership had been ignored during the Munich crisis and having little faith in the Allies' record of appeasement, Stalin signed the Nazi-Soviet Non-Aggression Pact on August 23, 1939. This pact divided Europe into zones of influence in the event that Poland was cut in two.

A German woman is paraded down a Munich street, calculatingly humiliated for having a sexual relationship with a Jew. Translated from the German, the sign that hangs from her neck reads: "I am a swine." Nazis considered Germans to be racially superior, and considered Slavs, gypsies and blacks to be inferior. At the bottom of this scale were the Jews, the most dangerous of the races, in part because they parasitically lived off the other races and weakened them. Declared Hitler: "All who are not of a good race are chaff." Seven documents were required to prove German descent: a birth or baptismal certificate, certificates for both parents, and certificates for all four grandparents.

The magnificent Fasanenstrasse Synagogue in Berlin was destroyed during Kristallnacht, *the "Night of the Broken Glass."* On November 9, 1938, anti-Jewish violence erupted throughout Germany, Austria and the Sudetenland. Within forty-eight hours, more than a thousand synagogues were burned. Ninety-six Jews were killed, 7,000 Jewish businesses were ransacked and looted, and Jewish cemeteries, hospitals, schools and homes were destroyed. Hitler had served notice to the Jews of what they might expect in his Third Reich.

As Nazi troops spread throughout Eastern Europe during the late 1930's, anti-Semitism began a rampant and sanctioned surge. In Rumania, Jewish university students were prevented from attending classes, Jewish lawyers were not allowed to practice, and a Jewish theater was bombed. In Yugoslavia, the editor of an anti-Semitic newspaper was tried and acquitted. In Czecho-slovakia, Jews were arbitrarily imprisoned for "sacrilege." In Lithuania, Jews were prevented from entering universities. In Hungary, Jews were prohibited from becoming lawyers, judges, school teachers or members of Parliament. And, in 1939, a bomb was thrown into a Budapest synagogue, killing one Jew and injuring scores of others.

In Poland during the 1930's anti-Semitism reached fever pitch through outrageous propaganda and outright slaughter. The Roman Catholic Cardinal Hlond declared in an open letter to the public: "It is true that the Jews are committing frauds, practicing usury, and dealing in white slavery." On March 9, 1936, the murder of three Jews in the village of Przytyk sent a shock wave of fear through Poland's three million Jews. A few days later, five Jews were murdered in the village of Stawy.

In August, 1937, there were 350 attacks on Jews, and in Katowice, bombs were thrown into Jewish-owned shops. Between 1935 and 1937, 79 Jews were killed and some 500 injured throughout Poland. Tens of thousands of Jews fled Poland.

As the situation deteriorated for Central and Eastern European Jewry, nothing could have predicted the force of the next development from Germany. Nothing to date compared with the violence of *Kristallnacht* (crystal night, or the night of the broken glass). A fancy name for the pogrom that erupted throughout the Reich on the night of November 9, 1938, *Kristallnacht* was intended to look like a spontaneous outburst of national anger over the killing of a German embassy official in Paris by Hershel Grynszpan, a Jewish youth, distraught over his parents' ejection from Germany. Nevertheless, it had been carefully and cynically orchestrated by the Nazis. The Gestapo warned local police units throughout the Reich that it was coming and told them not to interfere.

Within forty-eight hours, 91 Jews were killed, about 1,000 synagogues were burned, 7,000 Jewish businesses were vandalized and looted, and countless Jewish cemeteries, hospitals, schools and homes were destroyed. Thirty-thousand Jews were arrested; and the concentration camps at Dachau, Buchenwald and Sachsenhausen were expanded to accommodate them.

As a perverse finale to the bestiality of *Kristallnacht*, the Nazis demanded punitive reparations from the Jewish community. A fine of one billion reichmarks was imposed; all insurance payments were confiscated by the

State; and finally, the rubble of the synagogues and other ruined buildings had to be cleared by the Jews.

After assessing the fines, Hermann Göring said: "The swine won't commit another murder. Incidentally . . . I would not like to be a Jew in Germany."

Among the many things shattered on *Kristallnacht* was the illusion that Jews could survive in Nazi Germany. More repressive measures against Jews were soon put into effect. Jews were barred from schools and local authorities were given the right to impose curfews on them. By December, 1938, Jewish businesses were *aryanized* and Jews were denied access to most public places. In despair and desperation, the Jews tried to escape.

Although more and more Jews wanted to leave Europe, there was no place to go. Emigration to Palestine was severely limited by the British. Switzerland did not want to be overrun by Jews. The United States had a strict quota system, and had no provision for political refugees. The American Jewish community, splintered and powerless, was hesitant about bringing pressure to demand a more open refugee policy. American Jews were afraid of stirring up anti-Semitism.

As in Europe, it was a time of anti-Semitism in America. A Roper poll showed 60 percent of Americans thought Jews had "objectionable qualities." In virtually every poll, Jews were cited as posing a major threat to the community. A bill to allow 20,000 Jewish children from Germany to enter the country and be supported privately died in Congress. Isolationists argued that American children should come first. President Roosevelt never spoke in favor of the bill.

*The historic Bornestrasse Synagogue in Frankfurt, one of more than a thousand synagogues burned during the savage anti-Jewish violence of* Kristallnacht. *What appeared to be a spontaneous outburst of national anger sparked by the murder of a minor German embassy official in Paris by a Jewish youth had been carefully orchestrated by the Nazi regime. The cost of the broken window glass alone came to the equivalent of more than $2 million.*

BORNESTRASSE SYNAGOGUE, FRANKFURT (BEFORE AND AFTER)

Dorothy Thompson, the American journalist, wrote: "It is a fantastic commentary on the inhumanity of our times that for thousands and thousands of people, a piece of paper with a stamp on it is the difference between life and death."

Hitler's actions, however, were not stalled by debate, and on September 1, 1939, the German army invaded Poland. The world saw for the first time the devastating methods of *blitzkrieg*—lightning war. Before the invasion, Adolf Hitler told his generals to be harsh and remorseless, to act with brutality and

*Public humiliation of Jews became Nazi policy. Here Jews scrub the pavement under the supervision of members of the Hitler Youth. In order to "protect German blood and honor," the marriage of Jews and "citizens of German or kindred blood" was forbidden. So were sexual relations between Jews and Aryans. Only racial Germans were entitled to civil and political rights; Jews were merely subjects of the state. For the first time in history, Jews were persecuted not for their religious beliefs and practices, but because of their so-called racial identity, transmitted through the blood of their grandparents.*

*"Jews not permitted on the sidewalk," says this sign in both German and Polish. Many Jews, fearing for their lives, left Germany in the early days of the Nazi regime. Some moved to France only to be caught there when the country fell to Hitler's panzers. The more fortunate made it to America, Canada or other Western Hemisphere countries. The German-Jewish refugees included ordinary people—shopkeepers, artisans, doctors and lawyers—as well as distinguished writers, artists, scholars and scientists who represented the flowering of high German and European culture.*

close their hearts to pity. "It was," he said, "the stronger man who was always right." The Wehrmacht did not disappoint the Fuhrer. Within a week the German armored divisions and the Luftwaffe had wrecked the Polish Army.

Though pledged by treaty to come to the aid of Poland, Great Britain and France hesitated, talking of negotiating a return to peace. Not until September 3, two days after the attack, and after prodding by the House of Commons, did the Chamberlain government declare war.

The French were even more reluctant. By treaty, France was to launch a major offensive against Germany within days of an attack on Poland. Only twenty-three second-class divisions faced France's Maginot Line, where there were 110 German divisions. But France, perhaps remembering its horrendous casualties during World War I, did not attack.

The Poles were doubly betrayed when the Russians moved in behind them and grabbed the eastern half of their country. Poland surrendered in less than a month. It simply disappeared from the map and sank into a night of Nazi barbarism. No other occupied country would suffer so much.

# Chapter 5

*There is a desert inside me. My soul is scorched. I am naked and empty. There are no words in my mouth.*

**Elchanan Elkes, Kovno, Lithuania**

Under the Nazi onslaught, Europe collapsed. On April 9, 1940, Hitler invaded Denmark and Norway, subduing them in a matter of days. On May 10, German armies swept through Belgium and the Netherlands. The Netherlands fell in five days; Belgium in three weeks. A British army was trapped and had to be evacuated from the beaches of Dunkirk.

The demoralized French army offered little resistance to Hitler's Panzer divisions. Paris fell on June 13. An armistice divided France into two parts: the north occupied by Germany, parts of the South occupied by Italy, Hitler's ally. The rest of the south remained under French control, with Marshal Philippe Petain at the head of the Vichy government, a puppet of Germany.

The next step was the invasion of England. In preparation, the Luftwaffe launched massive bombing raids, but the Royal Air Force offered unexpectedly stiff resistance. Between July and October, the Luftwaffe lost 1,722 aircraft, the RAF 915. The invasion was called off.

With England out of reach, Hitler began to prepare for Operation Barbarossa, the code name for the invasion of the Soviet Union. On April 6, 1941, with Bulgaria and Romania already under German domination, Hitler invaded Greece and Yugoslavia. Both countries proved difficult to subdue, forcing Germany to postpone the invasion of Russia until late June and, subsequently, to fight in the deadly Russian winter.

Hitler insisted the invasion of the Soviet Union was necessary "to secure for the German people the land and the spoils to which they are entitled on this earth. Only thus shall we gain the *Lebensraum* which we need." There was more to it than that, however. "The war made possible," wrote Goebbels, "the solution of a whole series of problems that could never have been solved in peacetime."

For a while the German occupation forces in the West were on their best behavior, and the peace terms seemed relatively mild. Hitler insisted that he only wished to protect the neutrality of Scandinavia and the Low Countries. His armistice with France, while harsh, was not dishonorable.

Then the Germans set about bleeding the vanquished nations. France, Belgium, Norway and the Netherlands were made to pay the costs of occupation. The assessments were astronomically inflated. From 1940 to 1944, the French were made to pay the equivalent of $7 billion annually—ten times the cost of the military occupation. The annual assessment in Belgium exceeded the national budget.

The Germans took control of industry and other enterprises. Each country was forced to give up its resources. Denmark eventually furnished food for 8.4 million Germans in 1944. Belgium's iron and steel industry supplied 16 percent of the Reich's requirements. Norway produced aluminum for Hitler's war machine. France, Germany's traditional enemy, was the most exploited. A French general complained, "The Germans are treating France like a warehouse to be cleared at will."

The Reich also exploited the manpower of the conquered countries. The Waffen-SS recruited 125,000 soldiers in occupied Western Europe. In addition, some four million men and women from the western occupied countries, both prisoners of war and civilians, worked in Germany during the war. For the first two years, they were volunteers, more than a half-million in all. They were driven by the unemployment and economic chaos at home and the promise of better jobs and higher pay in Germany.

By the spring of 1942, volunteers no longer sufficed. The Russian campaign was consuming so much manpower and materiel that Hitler instituted a labor draft from the occupied countries. As the war dragged on, laborers in the occupied countries were tracked down and shipped off as assiduously as were Jews. Eventually nearly 600,000 laborers were drafted and shipped off to Germany.

Except for the Jews, the people of the occupied countries had a clear-cut choice: collaborate with the Germans or resist them. There was no middle ground. The rewards of resistance were intangible and remote, the dangers concrete and immediate. Most Europeans assumed that the war was all but over and that Germany had won. Although they mistrusted and resented the Germans, many people directed their anger at their own monarchs and governments which had fled into exile. Their sense of abandonment was heightened by appeals from their former leaders for further resistance when it seemed clear that to continue the conflict would only increase the catastrophe.

Throughout occupied Europe, collaborators turned in Jews who had managed to avoid arrest or who had escaped from incarceration. It was both easy and profitable to do so; collaborators who denounced Jews could receive in return food, goods, their own personal safety or simply perverted satisfaction. Many others who were not active collaborators acquiesced to what they saw happening around them, avoiding their eyes, telling themselves it was none of their business.

Others were indifferent to the plight of the Jewish Community and this indifference aided the Nazis. The Nazis depended on the seeming lack of concern shown by the Allied nations, who by 1942 were well aware of Nazi crimes. In the summer of 1939, England all but closed the doors of Palestine, a British protectorate, to Jewish refugees. The Jewish underground in Palestine organized its own rescue activities. It bought or rented boats and tried to bring Jews in illegally. Many times the boats were ordered returned to Europe.

Later, both Great Britain and the United States closed their doors to Jewish refugees. The United States only began its belated rescue efforts in January 1944, when Secretary of Treasury Henry Morganthau presented President Roosevelt with decisive new evidence of governmental inaction that Roosevelt knew would be politically explosive if it became public. The record of the Department of State has been described as the "abandonment of the Jews."

The Roman Catholic Church, which had vigorously protested Hitler's euthanasia policy, also did not speak out against the killing of the Jews. The Vatican was among the first to know of the genocidal programs. There were tens of thousands of priests in cities, towns and villages throughout Europe who saw Jews rounded up and deported to the camps. Some Jews even sought sanctuary from Church institutions, such as convents and monasteries. Authoritative information on the killings of Jews was sent to the Vatican by its own diplomats in March, 1942. Yet the Vatican remained silent.

The treatment of Jews in occupied territories followed a familiar pattern: first, Jews were categorized; then their property was confiscated; they were dismissed from civil service jobs and universities, and barred from most professions; their businesses were taken over and *aryanized.*; they were then isolated, forbidden to use public facilities, and forced to wear the Star of David. The final step was to assemble the Jews, first in large cities then in transit camps. From 1942 on, they were deported from the transit camps to the death camps in the east.

In Norway, Vidkun Quisling paved the way for deportations by reviving a long-dead provision of the constitution that banned Jews and Jesuits from the country. Of Norway's 1,700 Jews, 770 were sent to Auschwitz, and only 24 survived.

The Netherlands suffered the single greatest loss of Jews in Western Europe. Shortly after the occupation began, Jewish property and businesses were confiscated. Jews were expelled from the government and the professions. They were required to register with the authorities, forbidden to ride public transportation, and ordered to wear the yellow Star of David. A Jewish Council was set up to have prominent Jews help administer the nightmarish tangle of regulations and paperwork.

In September 1941, the Gestapo established in the Netherlands the final necessary link in the chain of bureaucracy—the Central Office for Jewish Emigration. Less than a year later, in July 1942, this office directed the first large deportations. Of the nearly 110,000 Jews sent to the camps from the Netherlands, only 5,000 would survive.

Out of Amsterdam came one of the most touching and best-known stories of the war. From July 1942, fifteen-year-old Anne Frank had been cooped up with her family and four other Jews in her father's former office building. On August 4, 1944, Dutch Nazi police discovered the door that led to their hiding place. They had been betrayed by an informer who received the equivalent of $1.40 for his information.

Seven months later, Anne Frank died of typhus in the Bergen-Belsen concentration camp. During the two years she had been in hiding, however, Anne had kept a diary, which was left behind in a heap of rubbish. Published shortly after the end of the war, The Diary of a Young Girl quickly became one of the best-selling books of all time.

In Belgium, the German occupation government apparently had little stomach for enforcing Himmler's Jewish policies, leaving the roundup and deportation to his own SS agents. About 24,000 Belgian Jews would die in the camps.

Of all the countries of occupied Europe, only Denmark rescued virtually all of its Jews. With a long tradition of tolerance, the Danes regarded the Jewish question as a problem for the whole nation. Danish Jews were accepted and respected, and regarded as Danes.

Danes were considered Aryans by the Germans. Their languages were related and the ties between the two countries had been close. After the occupation, the Danes were at first allowed to run their country without a great deal of interference, and Danish Jews were not persecuted. By 1943, they were no longer exempt from extermination. Plans for the deportation of Jews were leaked to Danish political leaders by their German sources.

Trouble was clearly coming. A list of Jews was confiscated from the Jewish community. On September 28, 1943, a German naval attaché, Georg Ferdinand Duckwitz, alerted a Danish political leader that the Jews were about to be rounded up. The Danish response was immediate. Farmers, fishermen,

Anne Frank, a Jewish girl who lived in Amsterdam with her family, kept a poignant diary of the war years. It was later published and became world famous. When the roundup of Dutch Jews began, friends hid the Franks and four others in a secret "annex" in what had been an office building. "In spite of everything," Anne wrote, "I still believe that people are good at heart . . ." Following capture by the Dutch Gestapo, Anne's mother died at Auschwitz. Anne and her older sister were sent to Bergen-Belsen. In March 1945, a month before the camp was liberated, Anne and her sister died. The only survivor was their father, Otto, who returned to Amsterdam after the war and found Anne's diary still on the floor of the hiding place where she had dropped it.

businessmen, taxi drivers, doctors and clergymen joined in a well-coordinated clandestine effort to spirit the Jews out of the country before they could be shipped off to the death camps.

On the eve of the Jewish New Year, synagogue services were cancelled and the Jewish community was told to go into hiding. They left Copenhagen and other Danish cities by train, bus, car and on foot. Hiding places were found in homes, hospitals and churches in coastal towns and on nearby farms. The Jews were to leave Denmark by sea.

Money had to be raised to rent fishing boats. Many individuals were able to pay for boats, the Jewish community was able to obtain a loan and many non-Jewish Danes donated money. During October 1943, 7,220 Jews left Denmark (along with 700 of their non-Jewish relatives) on fishing boats. Danish police came to the aid of the rescuers. Coast guard vessels acted as escorts. For two weeks, the boats ferried Jews across the narrow strait separating occupied Denmark and neutral Sweden.

More than 90 percent of the Jews in Denmark escaped deportation to death camps. When deportations began, only 464 Jews were left in Denmark, and they were transported to "the model ghetto" Theresienstadt. Of those deported, all but fifty-one lived through the war.

The Danish rescue experience did not end there. Jewish property was carefully protected. Homes and their contents were inventoried, and businesses were placed in trust. Torah scrolls and holy objects were stored in churches and returned intact to the Jewish community after the war.

The Danes showed their contempt for the Nazis in other ways, too. Mass demonstrations choked the city streets, and acts of sabotage were common. The Germans imposed curfews and began interning Danes in labor camps. These measures only fueled Danish resistance. On August 24, 1943, Resistance agents dynamited the Forum Exhibition Hall near Copenhagen just hours before it was to be rededicated as a German Army barracks.

The Danish experience was unique in Europe. King Christian X served as an example to his people by publicly wearing the Star of David to signify his identification with the Jews. Danes at every level of society, from fisherman to high government officials, have said they did not think they did anything special. They simply treated Jews as the neighbors they were.

France was a democratic nation and supposedly relatively free of anti-Semitism. Yet when France surrendered, many French people turned their backs on their Jewish countrymen and the many Jewish refugees present, and even informed on those in hiding. Half of the 350,000 Jews living in France when the Nazis invaded were recent émigrés. Half of the French Jews lived in Paris. The Germans had only 3,000 police in France, and needed French cooperation to move against the Jews.

During the first two years of Nazi occupation, the Vichy government in southern France aggressively put anti-Jewish laws into practice. French police participated in the deportations of Jews, which began in 1942. In six months 42,500 Jews were shipped to Auschwitz from the transit camp in Drancy. A third of those deported were from the unoccupied zone controlled by the Vichy government.

To earn German favor, the Vichy government enacted its own anti-Jewish laws, even going so far as to voluntarily round up some 4,000 Jewish orphans between the ages of two and twelve for deportation to the East. There were offers of help from people who could have hidden the children. But Vichy officials refused to listen to such pleas and the frightened children were put on trains bound for Auschwitz.

There were happy exceptions. A village in the south of France not far from Lyon, Le Chambon-sur-Ligon, became a haven for 5,000 Jews, many of them children. From the fall of France in June, 1940 until November, 1942, when Germany took over the entire country, the Lyon region was part of the unoccupied zone ruled by the collaborationist Vichy government.

The Protestant pastor of Le Chambon, André Trocmé, was instrumental in building a network of people in Le Chambon and neighboring villages who sheltered Jews in their homes. Local Catholic convents and monasteries also participated in the rescue effort.

The leaders were motivated by humanitarian feelings and religious beliefs. They were known as the *Responsables*—those who are accountable. Resistance in the village began slowly. At first, Trocmé urged village students to refuse to salute the Vichy flag. Then he refused an oath of unconditional loyalty to Pétain, the head of the Vichy government. His church was closed.

Magda Trocmé, the pastor's wife, recalled how Le Chambon was transformed into a place of refuge: "A woman knocked at my door one evening and she said she was a German Jew coming from northern France, and that she was in danger. She heard that in Le Chambon somebody could help her. Could she come into my house, I said, 'Naturally, come in, come in,' Lots of snow. She had a little pair of shoes, nothing." More and more refugees, many of them children, came to the town and were welcomed. Through the efforts of the *Responsables*, they managed to make it through the war there without being discovered. Despite such islands of protection, over 77,000 Jews from all of France were deported and died, either in camps or in detention.

Some 66,000 Jews lived in Belgium at the time of the Nazi invasion, primarily in Antwerp and Brussels, and were mostly refugees. Anti-Jewish laws were soon imposed. Some 26,500 Jews were sent to their death at Auschwitz.

Bulgaria was a strange case. The country became an ally of Hitler in return for the promise of receiving territory. After participating in the invasion of Yugoslavia and Greece, Bulgaria acquired Macedonia and Thrace. Then as Bulgaria drew closer politically to Germany, legislation was enacted restricting Jewish rights, although the country had no history of anti-Semitism. The anti-Jewish laws were criticized by intellectuals, political leaders, even the Holy Synod of the Bulgarian Eastern Orthodox Church.

When Germany pressed the Bulgarians in 1943 to deport Jews, it was met with stiff resistance. Some halfway measures were taken. The Jews of Sofia were expelled to the provinces, and Jewish men were sent to slave-labor camps. But there were no deportations to death camps. At the end of the war, Bulgaria's 50,000 Jews were still alive. Some sources say that King Boris personally gave the order to block the deportation, knowing that the Bulgarian people would not tolerate deportation of their fellow citizens.

The Jews of Finland came through the war without a loss. When pressed by Himmler in the summer of 1942 to implement anti-Jewish measures in

*Charred Hebrew prayer books from a destroyed synagogue in Bobenhausen, Germany. Nazi brutality in Germany and in conquered lands often struck first at Jewish places of worship. Today the sacred pages pictured here speak eloquently to visitors of the United States Holocaust Memorial in Washington, where they are now on display.*

1943, the Finnish foreign minister replied, "We prefer to die with the Jews; we shall never betray them." The country's small Jewish population was sent to Sweden for the duration of the war.

Help for the Jews came from unexpected quarters. Spain had friendly relations with Germany all during the war. Yet Spain saved more than 40,000 Jews by allowing them to enter the country. Arab nations were traditionally hostile to Jews. Yet King Muhammed V of Morocco protected some 300,000 Moroccan Jews from the pro-Nazi Vichy government that controlled his country. Japan, partner in the Axis with Germany, offered thousands of Jewish refugees sanctuary in the Chinese city of Shanghai, which Japan controlled at the time.

The Jews of Italy were also a special case. They could trace their roots to the era before the Roman conquest of Judea and the destruction of Jerusalem. Jews were living in Rome before St. Peter became the first Bishop of Rome, although in the 20th century, the Jews constituted only one-tenth of one percent of the population of Italy. They were fully assimilated, participants in Italian culture and society, and prominent in the professional and intellectual life of the country.

Fascist Italy was an ally of Germany. Yet as long as Benito Mussolini remained in power, no Jews were deported. Only after his fall in 1943 and the subsequent German invasion and occupation of the country, were Jews rounded up and deported. Even then, most were rescued as a result of efforts by the Italian people who protected them.

However, in 1938, to appease its German ally, Italy introduced racial laws. Jews could not teach or attend public schools. Foreign Jews could not establish residence, and those who had arrived after 1919 were deprived of their citizenship. The laws, however, were a pale imitation of the German racial laws, and the enforcement was lax. After Italy entered the war in June, 1940, refugee Jews were arrested and sent to internment camps. Native Italian Jews were subject to a mild form of house arrest.

Jews in Italian-occupied southern France were safer than those in Vichy, France. Deportations in Greece began only after the Italian forces left. Never warm allies of the Germans, Italians did not cooperate willingly with the Nazis in carrying out the Final Solution.

Mussolini was overthrown in 1943, but Germany invaded Italy and restored him as a puppet leader. With the Germans now in control, anti-Jewish policies were vigorously pursued. The roundup and deportation of Italian Jews began in October, 1943. The office of the Jewish community in Rome was plundered; its funds, library and archives confiscated. But the Jews took no steps to hide or protect themselves, believing that the Nazis would not deport the Jews of Rome in the shadow of the Vatican.

As it turned out, the Vatican had been informed of the planned deportations, but it failed to protest publicly or privately, before or after the fact. However, hundreds of priests and nuns did come to the aid of the Jews. Priests hid them in churches, monks and nuns opened monasteries and convents to them. The roundup of Italian Jews continued throughout the fall and winter of 1943-44. Italian police were pressed into service in the final stages of deportation. Despite all this, eight out of ten Jews escaped capture, with only 8,000 killed.

# Chapter 6

*Death lies in every street.*
*The children are no longer afraid of death.*
*In one courtyard, the children*
*played a game of tickling a corpse.*

## Emanuel Ringelblum
### Chronicler of the Warsaw ghetto

The Final Solution was the name given to an official Nazi program at a meeting in the Berlin suburb of Wannsee on January 20, 1942. The chairman of the meeting was Reinhard Heydrich, deputy to Heinrich Himmler, chief of the SS. He reminded the fifteen Nazi bureaucrats who attended that he had been authorized to organize a "complete solution to the Jewish question." The purpose of the meeting, he said, was to coordinate the efforts of all the relevant ministries, departments and agencies in implementing this task.

Heydrich presented a country-by-country breakdown of the eleven million Jews that he estimated still lived in Europe. According to the notes kept by Adolf Eichmann, his expert in Jewish affairs, Heydrich announced that all the Jews would be taken to camps in the East "for labor utilization." He declared, "doubtless a large part will fall away through natural reduction." adding that the survivors "will have to be dealt with appropriately."

The killing, of course, had already begun. By the time of the conference, more than a million Jews, Slavs and others had been shot, gassed or killed through overwork, starvation and disease. But most of these murderous efforts had been locally organized, particularly on the Eastern Front. The Wannsee meeting signaled the inauguration of a systematic, comprehensive and unprecedented program designed to exterminate an entire people.

Under the leadership of Himmler, the SS had been pressing mass emigration as a solution to the so-called Jewish problem since 1934. The central figure in these schemes was Adolf Eichmann, a meek-looking man who would come to embody the cold impersonality of the Nazi killing machine. A high school drop-out, he was a traveling salesman until he joined

An airtight metal door was fitted to each gas chamber. SS guards observed the killing through a small peephole. Shown is a casting of the door to the gas chamber at Majdanek. After the gas had done its work, the Sonderkommando was sent in to haul out the bodies. Gold teeth were extracted and women's hair was shaved. An elevator took the corpses to the crematorium located above the gas chamber.

the SS in 1933. He was given a clerical job in the SD, the new intelligence branch headed by Reinhard Heydrich, where he demonstrated a flair for bureaucratic detail.

Eichmann was not particularly anti-Semitic. In fact he had a Jewish mistress for awhile. Apparently he saw a chance for advancement in an organization that hated Jews. He was transferred to the SD bureau concerned with Jewish affairs. There, it is said, he picked up a little Yiddish and Hebrew, and found himself regarded as an expert. He was made the bureau's chief of Jewish emigration in 1937.

By this time, Himmler had decided that massive resettlement of Jews was necessary, and that Palestine might be the place to send them. The British, in the Balfour Declaration of 1917, had promised to create in Palestine a "national home for the Jewish people." The SS officially encouraged Zionist activities in Germany, and some 8,000 Jews annually emigrated to Palestine during the mid-1930s. Eichmann met in Berlin with an agent of the Haganah, the Jewish military underground in Palestine, to explore possibilities of stepping up the flow. He even made a trip to Palestine.

The Palestine solution didn't work out. Many German Jews remained reluctant to leave; others lacked the desire and the skills necessary to create a new life there. The British, faced with increased hostility between Jews and Arabs, limited Jewish immigration. Later, Hitler decided he didn't want to contribute to the creation of an independent state for his mortal enemies.

The rejection of the Palestine solution did not slow Eichmann's rise to power. The annexation of Austria brought nearly 200,000 more Jews into the Reich, and he was sent there to force them to emigrate. He set up the Central Office of Jewish Emigration in Vienna, bringing together under one roof all the government agencies involved in the emigration process. He put the paperwork on an assembly-line basis, and soon was processing papers for as many as 1,000 Jews a day.

Eichmann introduced other innovations. He forced wealthy Jews to subsidize the emigration of poor Jews. Jewish emissaries were sent abroad to raise funds for emigration and procure the foreign currency necessary to underwrite an emigrant's entry into another country. Eichmann's program of forced deportation, however, did not guarantee acceptance at the other end, and led to highly publicized international incidents of ships carrying Jewish refugees shuttling from port to port seeking to land their human cargo. Even so, Eichmann shipped out 50,000 Austrian Jews in six months, while Germany only deported 19,000 in a year.

On May 13, 1939, the SS St. Louis, a liner of the Hamburg-American Line, sailed from Germany for Cuba carrying 936 passengers, all but six of them Jews. Each had a landing permit to Cuba, but when the ship reached Havana on May 27, the Cuban government refused to honor the visas. Bribes were solicited at $500 a person. As the ship lay moored within yards of the shore, the price for the shipload was raised to $1 million.

The American Joint Distribution Committee (JDC), the Jewish organization responsible for relief and rehabilitation work overseas, was in a dilemma. To pay $1 million for the 930 Jews would lead other governments also to extort large sums. But there was increasing public pressure to meet the demand. The JDC continued to negotiate, while newspapers and the radio gave daily reports on the fate of the passengers. A telegram from the passengers was sent to President Roosevelt but went unanswered.

In New York, the JDC could find no other Latin American refuge. On June 5, an agreement was reached for all the refugees to land in Cuba if $453,000 was paid within twenty-four hours, but the JDC could not meet the deadline. When the *St. Louis* left Havana, the captain appealed to the United States for a haven, and as the ship sailed along the Florida coast the passengers could see the lights of Miami. The *St. Louis* set a course for return to Europe.

England, France, Belgium and the Netherlands admitted the passengers. Within months, the Nazis overran Western Europe leaving only the 288 passengers who were allowed to disembark in England as truly safe. Only a few of the others survived the Holocaust.

Meanwhile, Berlin was impressed with Eichmann's work. Göring ordered Heydrich to set up in Berlin a Reich Central Office of Jewish Emigration based on Eichmann's Vienna operation. But there were problems. The 350,000 Jews still in Germany were less able to leave; more than half were over forty-five years old; nearly one in five was sixty-five.

The greatest problem, though, was the worldwide glut of refugees, and the growing reluctance of other countries to let them in. More than 400,000 Jews had emigrated from Poland in the previous two decades. In June 1939, a few months after the establishment of the Reich Central Office, the SD reported a "growing tendency for other countries to lock their doors against Jewish immigration."

German Foreign Minister Joachim von Ribbentrop attempted to get neighboring countries to accept German Jews, but the climate of opinion had changed. He reported that France, a country which traditionally provided asylum for refugees, not only refused to accept any more Jews from Germany, but also wanted to ship 10,000 Jews already in France "somewhere else."

Forced emigration remained the ideal policy of the Nazi regime even with the outbreak of war and with the invasion of Poland in September 1939. But when Eichmann returned to Berlin the following month to take over the Reich

*A young survivor of the horrors of the "final solution" displays the identification number tattooed on his arm. On arriving at a concentration camp, persons not killed outright were stripped of every vestige of freedom and given uniforms that marked them as prisoners of the Reich.*

*Women being executed in occupied Poland. The Wannsee Conference of 1942 launched the systematic extermination of Europe's Jews, but Hitler had made his feelings about Jews clear long before that. As early as 1919, he wrote in his book Mein Kampf: "Rational anti-Semitism must lead to systematic legal opposition. Its final objective must be the removal of the Jews altogether." In many other instances Hitler outlined his goals and then proceeded to carry them out when the opportunity arose. Genocide, though, evolved gradually and in response to circumstances even Hitler could not have anticipated in his early days as a rabble-rouser.*

Central Office, he had to contend with the prospect of millions of Polish Jews. About two million Jews lived in the German-occupied zone; the rest in the eastern zone occupied by the Soviet Union. By the summer of 1940, Eichmann was hard at work on an emigration scheme designed to accommodate some four million European Jews.

Eichmann's preferred policy, the Madagascar Plan, was imaginative. According to the German Foreign Office, which proposed the plan after the fall of France in June 1940, France would cede the island of Madagascar to Germany. The German navy would have bases there, and the remainder of the island would become a reservation for Jews under the jurisdiction of

Himmler and the SS. The Jews would be held hostage there to influence the foreign policy of the United States.

Eichmann, who saw himself as governor of a new Jewish state, enthusiastically began to develop detailed plans. But the Madagascar Plan depended on the conclusion of a peace treaty with France, which in turn depended on an end of hostilities with England, because the Royal Navy controlled the sea lanes necessary for the transport of the great number of Jews to the island.

The Madagascar Plan was the last major attempt to solve the Jewish problem through emigration. While it was being considered, the machinery of a new solution was in motion.

This new solution was launched by Reinhard Heydrich on September 21, 1939, three weeks after the invasion of Poland. He told a meeting of his department heads in the Reich Central Security Office (an organization that included the Gestapo, SS, SD and the Criminal Police) that these measures were the "first steps in the final solution."

*Die Endlösung*, German for the final solution, had not yet taken on its horrendous meaning. One of the authors of the infamous Nuremberg Laws had used the phrase the year before to indicate that the legislation was only a temporary measure until the Jews were driven from Germany, and did not imply mass murder.

In Poland, the Reich annexed the northern and western portions, including provinces that Germany had given up under the Versailles treaty after World War I. The southern and eastern parts became an occupation zone, and designated the Government General of Poland. One million Jews from all over Europe and thousands of Gypsies and unwanted Polish gentiles were to be sent to the Government General. This would make room in the annexed area for ethnic Germans who were moving westward from the region under Soviet control.

In November 1939, the Jews in the Government General of Poland were forced to wear white armbands with a blue, six-pointed Star of David, two years before wearing the yellow star on a black background became compulsory for the Jews in Germany.

On December 1, 1939, the trains began to roll. An average of 3,000 Jews, Gypsies and Poles poured into the Government General a day, quickly overwhelming the capabilities of the new administration, which already had 1.4 million Jews under its jurisdiction. The governor, Hans Frank, protested to Göring, who ordered an end to the evacuations except those that were approved by Frank.

The Nazis began concentrating the Jews into ghettos that isolated them from the outside world. Many were surrounded by barbed wire or masonry walls. A ghetto typically was in the dirtiest, poorest and most crowded section of the city, where passage in and out was strictly controlled. In Warsaw, more than 400,000 Jews were crammed into the largest of the ghettos. A Nazi explained: "A race of lower standing needs less room, less clothing, less food and less culture . . ."

The day-to-day administration of the ghetto was performed by the Judenrat, or Jewish Council, usually appointed by the Germans. The Jewish Council recruited workers on demand for forced labor, and doled out the meager food that was supplied by the Germans. In the Warsaw ghetto, the food allocation eventually fell below 300 calories a day. The council also had to cope with epidemics of typhus, tuberculosis and the other diseases that flourished among the ill-fed people who were forced to live jammed together in filth. Death in the Ghetto was an ubiquitous and intimate companion.

By early 1941, Jews in Warsaw were dying of starvation at a rate of more than 2,000 a month. About 44,000 Jews in Warsaw died that year of all causes, more than a tenth of the ghetto population. "Death lies in every street," a member of the Jewish Council wrote. "The children are no longer afraid of death. In one courtyard, the children played a game of tickling a corpse."

In the early days of the occupation, the Nazi administrators in Poland viewed the ghettos as a step along the way to Madagascar. But Adolf Hitler had made his intentions clear. On January 30, 1939, he had told the Reichstag: "In my life I have often been a prophet, and most of the time I have been laughed at . . . Today I will be a prophet again. If international Jewry should succeed once more in plunging the peoples into a world war, the consequence will not be the Bolshevization of the earth and a victory of Jewry, but on the contrary, the destruction of the Jewish race in Europe."

Later in August, 1939, Hitler inaugurated two secret programs of systematic murder. They were carried out under the guise of euthanasia, or mercy killing. The subjects, not necessarily Jews but people with severe physical or mental problems were victims of the same notions of biological purity that were behind all of Hitler's racial ideas. The first program singled out deformed or retarded children. An estimated 5,000 such children were put to death during the next five years, usually by lethal injection, at special centers in twenty-one hospitals throughout Germany.

The other program, adult euthanasia, was more ambitious. "To administer to incurably sick persons a mercy death," Hitler authorized the establishment of the Committee for the Scientific Treatment of Severe, Genetically Determined Illness. The program bore the code name T-4, for the address of the agency's headquarters, an inconspicuous villa at Tiergartenstrasse No. 4 in a suburb of Berlin.

*A portrait of the Holocaust's loathsome tragedy: human bodies piled up, awaiting cremation at Buchenwald. Victims' faces are frozen in death, some with expressions of terror, others with expressions of relief.*

Doctors, including Hitler's personal physician, Dr. Karl Brandt, selected the victims from lists submitted by institutions. Those selected were transported to one of six killing centers established in abandoned prisons and asylums where they were ushered into a tiled chamber disguised as a shower room. Carbon monoxide gas was piped in, subsequent cremation destroyed any evidence. The family of the deceased received an urn of ashes and a letter of condolence attributing the death to natural causes.

People read the unexpected death notices in the newspapers with skepticism. People who lived near the killing centers noticed the smoke pouring from the chimneys of the crematoriums. In Hadamar, near one of the centers, children ran after the buses with the blacked-out windows shouting, "There goes the murder box again." Prominent clerics began to attack the program from the pulpit, even though among the German people, the program received a broad level of public support.

In September 1941, after more than 70,000 had been killed, Hitler ordered the termination of T-4. The killing of the handicapped and mentally ill continued in the new killing centers in the East, where, as inmates of concentration camps, the victims were certified as insane and put to death in the camp's own newly installed gas chamber.

T-4 was the unwitting pilot program for mass murder, and the apparatus of destruction was taking shape. The executioners were trained, the technology proved, the procedures worked out. Gas-chamber crews had even learned to turn a profit for the Third Reich by extracting gold-filled teeth from the corpses. Many of the doctors who participated in the T-4 program would go on to work in the death camps.

# Chapter 7

*Here we see things no one has ever seen before . . .*
*We stand and look on.*

## SS Sergeant Felix Landau

The invasion of Poland was the first concrete evidence that Adolf Hitler was serious about creating a racially pure society in the East by eliminating its native population. It seemed that from the very beginning, the Nazi invaders went out of their way to kill civilians. Hitler had told his military commanders. "The aim is not the arrival at a certain line, but the annihilation of living forces." He authorized them to kill "without pity or mercy, all men, women and children of Polish descent or language. Only in this way can we obtain the living space we need."

The resulting carnage was stupefying in its senseless cruelty. No one was safe, not pedestrians on the streets of Warsaw nor shepherds tending their flocks in remote fields. In Bydgoszcz, the "first victims of the campaign were a number of Boy Scouts . . . who were set up in the marketplace against a wall and shot," reported an Englishwoman who was living there at the time. Next came a priest, gunned down as he rushed into the square to administer last rites to the boys.

No Polish city or town was spared. The American ambassador to Poland, Anthony J. Drexel Biddle, Jr., reported that it seemed to be Germany's intention "to terrorize the civilian population and to reduce the number of child-bearing Poles, irrespective of category."

The reason behind this slaughter was Hitler's dream of *Lebensraum*, the space where a biologically pure German empire could be built; an empire with no room for the contaminating presence of racially inferior native populations. To Hitler, both the Jews and the Slavs were vermin that had to be cleared from the prospective German space.

Hitler made a critical distinction between the Jews and the Slavs. Nazis looked on Jews as creatures of mythic dimensions, responsible for every evil

*A Nazi officer looks on as a man is dragged off by two civilians during a roundup of Jews in Lvov, Poland, in July 1941. In Poland, the Soviet Union and other countries where anti-Semitism had flourished for centuries, many civilians willingly cooperated with the Germans in locating and rounding up Jews to be sent to the ghettos. Informers were a dime a dozen. The Polish ghettos were set up quickly but efficiently. By 1942, all the two million Jews of German-occupied Poland were confined to ghettos, living in hiding, or on the run. At first some ghettos were relatively open and Jews had little difficulty going in and out. But just before the final deportations all ghettos were sealed. The Germans considered the ghettos captive city-states, holding pens for a subjugated population with no rights. Jewish labor was to be exploited, goods and property to be confiscated.*

from prostitution to capitalism and Marxism. The Slavs (which to the Germans included the Czechs, Poles, Slovenes, Croats, Slovaks and Serbs, as well as the hundred or so ethnic groups in the Soviet Union) were another matter. They were *Untermenschen*, primitive, stupid creatures who were barely one rung above animals on the evolutionary ladder.

The Jews, the Germans believed, represented the greater danger. They should be uprooted and eliminated as quickly as possible by whatever means available. The Slavs were a threat only because they inhabited land coveted by Germany. Slavs, with some exceptions, were not marked for immediate extinction. The Czechs, whose country became a German protectorate in 1939, were generally spared, and Hungarians, Rumanians and Bulgarians, whose territories were strategically located or contained vital war industries, actually became wartime allies.

Heinrich Himmler created a network of agencies and bureaus to handle matters concerned with race, ethnicity and emigration. One of the largest was the *Volksdeutsche Mittlestelle* (VOMI), founded in 1936 to serve as the liaison between the Nazi party and the resettled 1.2 million ethnic Germans who were living in central and eastern Europe. In the SS, the Race and Settlement Office monitored the racial purity of SS candidates and their potential brides, studied rural settlement techniques and devised plans for the establishment of German colonies in the East.

In October, the *Wehrmacht*, the German Army, was relieved of the responsibility of administering the conquered Polish territories. With the country divided into the annexed western provinces and the Government General farther east, the stage was set for a full-scale attempt to implement *Lebensraum*.

The SS set up the Reich Commission for the Strengthening of Germanism (RKFDV) to plan and carry out colonization of conquered eastern territories. Slavic inhabitants would be cleared out and Germans settled in their place. Himmler was given a new title, *Reichskommissar* for the Strengthening of Germanism, and the task of evicting millions of Poles.

First, the Poles were classified according to their occupations, social status and attitudes toward the Germans. Scheduled for immediate removal were three groups: Poles who had settled in the area after 1918; Poles who had worked for the Polish nationalist cause; and Poles who were considered intelligentsia—teachers, physicians, landowners, writers, the clergy; along with anyone who had ever attended a secondary school. These people were considered a potential source of opposition to Nazi rule, and constituted a living refutation of Nazi claims of the subhuman status of all Poles.

Evictions were swift and brutal. An SS detachment would serve a family an eviction order. Often they were given only twenty minutes to pack a suit-case, and tidy their houses for the new occupants. All their luggage could weigh no more than a hundred pounds. The family could not bring valuables, not even wedding rings and gold-rimmed spectacles. Everything else was left for the incoming German settlers. Anyone who objected was killed.

The deportees were taken to transportation. Young, strong Poles were sent to Germany as slave laborers. Others were loaded onto freight trains and taken east to the Government General, where they were simply dumped in open fields and left to their own devices. Many died on the way. Jammed into unheated cattle cars in midwinter and often deprived for days of food and water, they died by the hundreds of exposure, malnutrition and asphyxiation.

Some Poles, left behind in anticipation of a temporary need for manpower, were deliberately treated with brutality to turn them into nothing more than dependable slaves. Polish men under the age of twenty-eight and women under twenty-five were not allowed to marry—one of several measures designed to reduce the Polish birth rate. All schools and most churches were shut down. Poles could not enter any of the professions.

Hans Frank, the Nazi governor-general of Poland, was told by Hitler that his ultimate job would be to finish off the Poles for good when they were no longer needed as slaves. Frank relished the assignment. "It is our aim that the very concept of Poland be erased for centuries to come," he vowed. "Neither the republic, nor any other form of Polish state will ever be reborn."

Frank ordered the destruction of monuments, statues, shrines, libraries and theaters. Works by Polish artists were either confiscated or destroyed. Any expression of patriotism, such as the showing of the Polish flag or the singing of the Polish anthem, was a capital offense. A Pole could be shot for not doffing his hat or yielding the sidewalk to an approaching German. Children were killed for making anti-German statements. Waves of arrests and liquidations killed hundreds of Poles every month. The sight of people being shot in the street became commonplace.

Poles were packed off to the concentration camps that sprang up all over German-occupied Poland. By the end of 1940, at least fifty camps were in the Government General alone. The original purpose was to get the most labor out of the prisoners at the least possible investment in food and upkeep. But even before the first large-scale gassings began in late 1941, incarceration in a concentration camp usually ended in death.

A Polish Catholic who was in the inaugural transport of 756 prisoners to Auschwitz in June, 1940 later calculated that the average life expectancy in the Polish camps was three weeks. Prisoners who lived much longer than that were often executed on the assumption that they must be stealing food. Ultimately, so many Poles were sent to concentration camps that virtually every family had a member who had died in one.

Paradoxically, during the first two years of Nazi rule, Christian Poles were more exposed than Jews to arrest, deportation and death. Jews were herded into ghettos to await the final determination of their fate. By June 1941, as final plans for the invasion of the Soviet Union were being made, some 30,000 Jews had already perished—about 20,000 from starvation and disease

*Awaiting deportation to a death camp, a young Jewish man in the Lodz ghetto contemplates his fate. His head has been shaved, his few belongings are in his shoulder bag, and a Star of David has been sewn on his coat. Like many deportees, this group appears apprehensive but resigned. Undoubtedly they know something of the horror that awaits them but, understanding the futility of resistance, choose to go with peace and dignity.*

in the Warsaw and Lodz ghettos alone, the rest in labor camps, street massacres, reprisal actions and individual shootings. But Jews had not yet been the target of any deliberate, systematic extermination effort. The German invasion of the Soviet Union would mark a critical turning point in the Nazi policy toward the Jews.

Hitler made sure his commanders understood that the coming conflict was not merely between states, but a battle to the finish between two opposing world-views. The "Jewish-Bolshevik" intelligentsia, he declared, were as much the enemy as was the Red Army. And as all Jews were members of this conspiracy, all Jews would have to be exterminated.

The Jews would be the responsibility of the SS, which would follow the army into the Soviet Union, and assume control of conquered territories and their inhabitants. In a departure from usual military procedure, a force of SS would actually accompany the invading army. Small, mobile units called *Einsatzgruppen* would rid the freshly taken territories of their undesirable civilian elements.

As the invasion approached, Reinhard Heydrich met with Eduard Wagner, quartermaster general of the *Wehrmacht*, to determine how the army and the SS could carry out their assignments simultaneously without getting in each other's way. They agreed that the *Einsatzgruppen* were to take their orders from the SS, but would be subject to army discipline. The army was to control their movement and supply quarters, rations, gasoline and communications.

A battalion-sized *Einsatzgruppe* would be attached to each of the four army groups that would attack along a 1,350-mile front. Most of the troops came from the Waffen SS, the Order Police and the Criminal Police. The police were chosen because they had demonstrated exceptional callousness and brutality; the SS men as punishment for a poor performance in the past.

*A Lithuanian guard strikes a Jew with his cane during a roundup in Riga, Lithuania, in the summer of 1941. When Hitler launched the invasion of the Soviet Union, German troops quickly seized the Baltic states of Latvia, Lithuania and Estonia and began rounding up the Jews. Local residents could see what was happening, but most did nothing to intervene. They were terrified. They knew that what was happening to the Jews one day might happen to them the next. The SS often encouraged the local population to conduct pogroms, particularly in Lithuania and Latvia, where anti-Semitism was endemic. The mobile killing units were so busy that local collaborators volunteered for this work.*

The officers, however, were among Germany's best-educated young professionals, and nothing in their backgrounds suggested sociopathic or criminal tendencies. Many were lawyers in their civilian lives, and their numbers included a physician and a professional opera singer.

As the date of the invasion grew near, the *Einsatzgruppen* officers were given spirited talks to make them enthusiastic about the acts they were expected to perform. During one briefing, Himmler addressed them personally, stressing the importance of eliminating Jews and Communist functionaries.

When Operation Barbarossa began on June 22, five million Jews lived in the Soviet Union. Most were concentrated in the sections overrun by the German *blitzkrieg* that summer. Every day, thousands more Jews found themselves trapped behind the German lines. To find and kill them, the *Einsatzgruppen* were divided into company-sized detachments called *Einsatzkommandos*. These units would enter a town and start rounding up civilian targets—Jews and Communist leaders—working from information supplied by military intelligence and local collaborators.

The victims were assembled, marched off somewhere out of sight of the local populace, and executed. Small Jewish communities of a few hundred to a few thousand could be slaughtered in a single day. In larger communities, such as Vilna, Lithuania, where there were 57,000 Jews, they were herded roughly into makeshift ghettos, from which they later were taken in groups to execution sites. Those who managed to escape the first wave of fast-moving killer squads were often eliminated by SS crews that came in later to administer the captured territories.

*An elderly man stands in front of a train bound for a death camp from Iasi, Rumania, probably wondering how he managed to survive while younger men, their corpses crowding the freight car, died along the way. Rumania was an ally of Germany in the invasion of Russia, and within days of the invasion, a massive pogrom took place in the northern Rumanian town of Iasi. At least 8,000 Jews were killed and thousands like the man in the photograph were deported in sealed trains and sent to Calarasi, some 300 miles away. Most of the human cargo perished from hunger and dehydration in the summer heat. Before the journey was over, 2,544 people had died.*

*A German soldier takes aim at a Jewish mother and child during a massacre of Ivangorod Jews during the Russian campaign. Nearby, Jews are being forced to dig their own graves. This photograph has a curious history. Enclosed in a letter written by a German soldier on the Eastern Front and posted to Germany, it was intercepted in the Warsaw post office by members of the Polish Home Army who kept surveillance over the mail. An inscription on the back of the photo reads: Ukraine 1942, Jewish Aktion, Ivangorod.*

The Germans were assisted in many areas by local anti-Semites, who not only helped round up Jews, but enthusiastically joined in the killings. As an *Einsatzgruppe* unit arrived in Kaunas, Lithuania, local partisans were still fighting Red Army troops who had occupied their country only a year earlier. When the Soviets retreated, the German commander persuaded the Lithuanian chief to help round up the Jews. The partisans acted with such fervor that within a few days they had killed some 5,000 Jews.

The speed of the German advance stunned the Jews. Bewildered and un-armed, they could not mount an effective resistance. Ironically, in the early weeks of the campaigns, the Jews were shocked that the Germans, of all people, should be doing such things. The Jews historically regarded Germany

*An SS officer executes partisans in Minsk in October 1941 during the Russian campaign. The hanged woman is Masha Bruskina, a Jew, whose crime was smuggling false documents to a prison camp for Soviet prisoners of war. At first many Ukrainians, tired of Stalin's repressive regime, welcomed the German troops. The Germans, however, treated them as* Untermenschen, *or subhumans, and they soon learned to fear the occupiers they once embraced.*

as a bastion of culture and enlightenment compared to the medieval religious hatreds of Russia. Many of the older Jews, remembering the courtesy and civility of the Germans who had occupied Russia in World War I, had looked forward to the arrival of the Germans.

"The Jews are remarkably ill informed about our attitude toward them," an SS intelligence officer reported. "They do not know how the Jews are treated in Germany, or for that matter, in Warsaw. They believe that we shall leave them in peace if they mind their own business and work diligently." The *Einsatzgruppen* exploited this attitude. Sometimes they would enter a village, contact the rabbi, and ask politely for Jewish volunteers. Then they would march the group off to be executed and come back for more.

*A Jew is executed by a member of an SS mobile killing squad near Vinnitsa, Ukraine in 1942. Witnessing the slaying are members of the German Army, the German Labor Service and the Hitler Youth. In Soviet territory, mass killing became operational policy. Accompanying the army were small units of SS and police called Special Action Squads, or Einsatz-gruppen. In Poland, the squads rounded up Jews, who then were forced into ghettos. In the Soviet Union their assignment was simpler: kill any Jews they could find in the territory taken by the army.*

A pattern developed. The Jews were assembled and taken to the killing site a small number at a time. The soldiers were reassuring so that their victims wouldn't panic. At the site, a mass grave was prepared. The Jews were handed shovels and told to start digging. When the grave was ready, they were ordered to surrender their money and other valuables. Often, just before they were lined up on the edge of the ditch to be shot, they were ordered to strip, to further break their will to resist.

Some resisted anyway. Rivka Yosselevska, who somehow survived a massacre at Zagrodski, near Pinsk, said, "Our father did not want to undress. He did not want to stand naked. They tore the clothing off the old man, and he was shot." In the next few minutes, Rivka stood frozen, holding her daughter in her arms, and watched her entire family die. First her mother was shot, then her eighty-year-old grandmother and the two children she was holding. Next her aunt, also with children in her arms, was killed. Then came Rivka's two sisters, and finally it was her turn. "I felt the German take the child from my arms. The child cried out and was shot immediately. Then he aimed at me. He aimed the revolver at me and ordered me to watch, then turned my head around and shot me. Then I fell into the pit, amongst the bodies." Rivka, wounded in the head, played dead and crawled away after the soldiers left.

Some commanders insisted on mass fire from a distance to protect their troops from possible charges of personal responsibility for any individual deaths. And some were concerned about the psychological effect of the killings on their troops. Unless the killings were carried out in a correct military manner, one commander explained, "the psychic burden would have been too much for the execution commando."

But things often got out of hand, particularly when local police or militia were allowed to deal with the Jews in their own way. An SS sergeant wrote in his diary about what greeted him when he drove into Drogobych to find the town turned into an abattoir: "The streets tell of murder. Hundreds of Jews with bloodstained faces, with bullet holes in the head, broken limbs, gouged-out eyes, run ahead of us. One of the Jews carries another one, who is bleeding to death. We drive to the prison. Here we see things no one has ever seen before. It is absolutely impossible to describe them. Two soldiers stand at the entrance to the prison. Wielding sticks as big as fists, they lash furiously at the crowds. Jews are being pushed out from inside. Covered with blood, they collapse on top of one another—they scream like pigs. We stand and look on."

Heinrich Himmler toured the East to see for himself how the *Einsatzgruppen* program was progressing. At the SS operations center at Minsk, a demonstration was arranged for his benefit. A hundred prisoners were taken out to an open grave, ordered to jump in a few at a time and told to lie face down. Each group in turn was then shot from above. Himmler, who apparently had never seen people shot before, stepped up to get a better look at the killing.

"While he was looking on," an observer recalled, "Himmler got a splash of brains on his coat. I think they also splashed into his face. He went very green and pale. He wasn't actually sick, but he was heaving, and he turned around and swayed."

After regaining his composure, Himmler gave an impromptu speech. The men saw, he said, how deeply affected he had been by what he had just seen. It was a hateful business, and he would not like it if Germans did such things gladly. But he assured the men that they were doing their duty in accordance with a higher law. Mankind must decide what is harmful and defend itself. Vermin must be destroyed.

Himmler later spoke to his commanders about finding a less traumatic method of killing than shooting. An experiment was made in which dynamite was used to blow up mental patients, but the results were unsatisfactory. Technicians came up with a more successful method of killing—the gas van. Large trucks were modified so that their poisonous carbon-monoxide exhaust fumes would be conducted to their sealed interiors.

Each *Einsatzgruppe* received two such vans, and others were sent to Poland. But despite their effectiveness, they were simply too small. Their capacity was less than fifty people. This was inadequate for the mass murders being committed daily in the East and for the even more massive killings Berlin was planning.

The most practical method of extermination still was to march victims away a few at a time and shoot them where their bodies would fall into ditches and ravines. When well organized, this was an extremely effective method, as it would soon be demonstrated near Kiev in a deep natural cleft in the earth known as Old Woman's Gully—Babi Yar.

# Chapter 8

*I have a feeling that great things are happening, that what we have dared is of great importance.*

## Mordecai Anielwicz
### resistance leader, Warsaw ghetto

The conquest of the Soviet Union progressed rapidly. By mid-September, 1941, panzer divisions captured Kiev, the country's third largest city, then pulled out and rolled toward Moscow, their next objective. The SS, in collaboration with the local police, took over the city government. Less than two weeks later a notice appeared ordering all Kiev's Jews to report the next day to the old Jewish cemetery on the outskirts of the city not far from a railroad station. The notice suggested the Jews would be resettled.

The Jews started leaving their homes before dawn so that they could get seats on the train. The streets soon were packed with people loaded down with bundles, or pushing wheelbarrows, handcarts and baby carriages. It was afternoon before they reached the cemetery. As they approached they could hear the sound of machine-guns, but few believed the Germans would shoot innocent civilians. On arrival, they were told to set their belongings aside, then they were divided into groups of ten and marched away.

As the small groups approached their still unknown destination, the soldiers along the path became more numerous, until they stood shoulder to shoulder, creating a corridor about five feet wide. The soldiers shouted, *"Schnell, Schnell!"*—hurry, hurry! and beat the Jews with rubber truncheons. The screams of the victims blended with the shouts and jeers of the soldiers and the barking of guard dogs.

Finally the terrorized Jews arrived at a clearing filled with Ukrainian police, who seized them and shouted at them to undress. Those who hesitated were forcibly stripped. Then little groups were led naked through a narrow gap in an earthen bank to an area from which came the steady bursts of gunfire. All went quickly except when women clung tightly to their children, or fumbled as they tried to help them undress. This was the beginning of the savage slaughter at Babi Yar.

Nearby was a group of some fifty people who had persuaded the guards that they were not Jewish, and had been caught in the crowd. As night fell, a car arrived and a German officer stepped out. Told about the group, he barked, "Shoot them! If even one of them gets away, we won't get a single

*During a roundup of 420 Jews in Bielefeld, Lithuania, in 1941, women board a train to be taken to a concentration camp. Jews were ticketed as regular passengers, although they were transported as cattle, mainly in freight cars. The SS used travel agents to book one-way passage to the camp at the rate of four Pfennigs (pennies) per kilometer of track they would travel. Children under ten rode for half fare; those under four rode free. A group rate of half the usual third-class charge was introduced for deportations of more than 400 people. There were basically three forms of deportation. First, Jews were deported from their homes to ghettos or transit camps. Then they were deported from small to large ghettos. Then, from 1942 on, they were deported to one of the six major death camps—Auschwitz/Birkenau, Majdanek, Chelmno, Treblinka, Belzec and Sobibor.*

*Two children huddle together in the Warsaw ghetto. The murder of a million Jewish children was the ultimate crime of the Holocaust, a deliberate attempt to destroy the Jewish future. The children, the most vulnerable of the victims, were caught up in a web of incomprehensible events. Many first felt the sting of persecution in the classroom or schoolyard. In Poland and Eastern Europe, children went with their parents into the ghettos, often becoming beggars or smugglers. Later they were sent to the concentration camps with their parents. Parents who refused to be separated from their children were immediately sent to the gas chambers. Only the able-bodied and the unencumbered could hope to survive.*

Jew tomorrow." Not taking time to have them strip, the guards herded them through the gap. They emerged on the brow of a deep ravine. Across the ravine was a line of machine guns. Far below, the floor of the ravine was carpeted with bloody, naked bodies.

Just as the order to fire came, Dina Mironovna Pronicheva, an actress from the Kiev Puppet Theater, hurled herself into the ravine, diving straight into the mass of corpses. She lay perfectly still, her eyes closed, her arms outstretched. Beneath her she felt steady undulating motion. Many of the victims were still alive, and the whole mass gently stirred.

Soldiers shone flashlights into the pit, shooting at any sign of life. Some came down into the pit. One SS man stumbled over Dina, yanked her limp form up for a closer look, then dropped her back down, gave her a sharp kick and turned away. After the soldiers clambered out of the pit, sand began thudding down on the bodies. When the sand started getting in her mouth, Dina clawed herself free and slowly made her way to the gully wall, silently climbing out under cover of darkness.

*German troops round up Polish Jews in Kerceli Square in Warsaw. The German brutal occupation of Poland focused on Warsaw. Unknown numbers were shot down in Gestapo roundups and in reprisal for guerrilla actions. Often, the homes of suspects were dynamited. "Warsaw shall not be rebuilt," said Rudolf Hess, the deputy führer, echoing Hitler's order. Between 1940 and 1942, an estimated 100,000 Jews died from starvation, disease or execution in the city. In July 1942, a sweep of the ghetto rounded up 300,000 more Jews for transportation to camps. Most were sent to the Treblinka death camp. In January 1943, Himmler ordered an end to the "resettlement program," and SS troops entered the ghetto to make Warsaw "Jew-free," setting the stage for the heroic uprising in the ghetto.*

Dina Pronicheva lived to tell of her ordeal. But on that day and the next, 33,771 Jews died at Babi Yar. Babi Yar was also the final resting place for Gypsies and Soviet prisoners of war. Some 200,000 would die at Babi Yar during the two years of Nazi occupation. In August 1943, the decomposing bodies were excavated and burned in a furnace built of granite tombstones taken from Kiev's Jewish cemetery.

The Germans went to great lengths to keep massacres like Babi Yar secret. Nothing about them was published, and soldiers and others who took part were ordered never to discuss them. In February, 1942, Reinhard

Heydrich told a group of regional SS commanders that the extermination of the Jews was going so smoothly that the local Russians barely noticed what was going on.

But no one in the occupied East could have failed to see what was going on. They had seen the Jews marched off and heard the guns firing. The local police who helped the Germans kill the Jews told their families and neighbors. And there were occasional survivors, like Rivka Yosselevska and Dina Pronicheva.

The slaughter of the Jews caused a sensation among the German troops. The killing sites were off-limits to ordinary soldiers, but many slipped away to witness the executions. They took pictures, wrote letters, told other soldiers. The news began to filter back to Germany.

Pogroms were not new in Russia. Jewish villages had been sacked for centuries. The Soviet people under Stalin knew all about death on a massive scale. But no one had ever seen anything quite like the methodical extermination now taking place. Most Russians had no qualms about killing Jews, but the reality of what was going on left many of them appalled. They began to ask one another, "When will it be our turn?"

The occupied territories were divided into the Theater of Military Operations and the Military Administrative Zone. The latter had a civilian administration that answered to a new agency, the Reich Ministry for Eastern

*Emanuel Ringleblum was an active force in the Warsaw ghetto. A trained historian, he formed a group to painstakingly document life in the ghetto, in the belief that the historical records of a doomed community must be preserved. Before the war, he had worked for the American Jewish Joint Distribution Committee in Poland and was sent to deal with refugees stranded at the Polish border. In the ghetto he kept a daily chronicle. Hidden on the Aryan side after the final destruction of the ghetto, Ringelblum was discovered and shot by the Nazis in March 1944.*

Occupied Territories. It consisted of two sections: "Ostland"—the Baltic States and Belorussia—and "Ukraine"—the bulk of the Ukraine proper and the part of eastern Poland that had earlier been occupied by the Soviets.

The fate of the people in these areas depended in large measure on the Nazi conception of where they fell on the racial scale. For example, the Estonians were believed to be racially German; Latvians and Lithuanians were considered to be partially Germans. This meant that their lives would be spared. In other parts of the Soviet Union, the natives were considered subhuman and subject to deportation to Asiatic Russia, slavery, or extermination.

The forty-million Slavic inhabitants of the Ukraine hated their Soviet occupiers and their Jewish neighbors, so much so that they could have been the Nazis' natural allies. Soon, however, they too were the target of brutal measures. The rich farmland of the Ukraine made it the Soviet breadbasket

*In a Polish ghetto, a young Jewish boy plays his violin in the hope that passersby will reward him with a coin or two. There were few coins to spare, however. The Germans sealed off the ghettos with walls and wire. Jews trying to escape were shot. Property was confiscated, synagogues were destroyed. Jews were forced to work for the Germans but were not paid for their labors. The ghettos were marked by squalor, disease, starvation and the stench of raw sewage. As bad as it was, however, life in the ghetto was preferable to the death that awaited Jews in the camps.*

*Jews from Lublin, Poland, are hustled along by an SS trooper to the train that will take them to the camp at Sobibor. The Germans there went to great lengths to make the Jewish prisoners believe that they were being resettled. At Sobibor, inmates disguised as railroad porters helped the prisoners with their luggage and gave them checks for reclaiming it. The Germans even passed out postcards and asked the Jews to write home to report their safe arrival. A few skilled craftsmen along with the strongest looking young people were pulled from the ranks for the camp's work force. The others were taken to the killing grounds out of earshot of the other Jews.*

and the most coveted territory in the German *Lebensraum* plan. Hitler had no intention of sharing it with those he regarded as "helots, subhumans and monkeys."

The administrator of the Ukraine, Erich Koch, told his subordinates in September 1941: "I am known as a brutal dog. That is why I was chosen Reichskommissar. Our task is to suck from the Ukraine all the good we can get hold of without consideration of the feelings or the property of the Ukrainians. I am expecting from you the utmost severity toward the native population."

Koch planned to depopulate the Ukraine by murdering the Jews and Gypsies, then decimating the remaining population through famine,

*Jews are rounded up during the Warsaw ghetto uprising. In the summer of 1942, some 300,000 Jews were shipped from Warsaw to the Treblinka death camp. Finally, when only 55,000 remained in the ghetto, the decision was made to resist. The Germans had planned to liquidate the ghetto in three days, but fighting began on April 19, 1943, the second night of Passover, and continued for more than a month. Of the Jews captured, 7,000 were shot, 7,000 were transported to Treblinka, and 15,000 were shipped to the concentration camp at Lublin. German troops captured nine rifles, fifty-nine pistols, several hundred hand grenades and mines. German losses included sixteen dead and eighty-five wounded. The uprising was a turning point in Jewish history; Jews had resisted the Nazis with armed force.*

deportations and massacres triggered by the slightest provocation. In November 1941, food supplies bound for Ukrainian cities were diverted to the Reich and the German army.

The Ukraine was in the grip of the institutionalized terrorism that had earlier engulfed Poland. No one could be sure he or she would be spared sudden, arbitrary death. A notice was posted in Kiev informing the citizenry that a hundred residents had been shot in retaliation for an act of sabotage. Two weeks later, an order was issued declaring that 300 hostages would be shot for the next such incident.

The flood of directives covered a bewildering variety of infractions, from not turning in felt boots to failing to inform on Jews. Failing to observe the

*As Nazi panzer divisions drove into the Soviet Union along a 2,000-mile front, SS Special Action Squads followed the army, killing any Jews they could find along the way. Jews were easy to find. Nearly nine of ten lived in large cities in the path of the rapidly advancing armies. The mobile killing units moved swiftly, taking the Jewish population by surprise and leaving communities too paralyzed to act. Those rounded up—men, women and children—were marched to the outskirts of the city and shot. Their bodies then were buried in hastily dug ditches.*

most trivial rule could mean summary execution. Curfew violators were shot on the spot, their bodies left on the sidewalks. The most law-abiding citizen might still be seized and executed in the aftermath of an anti-German incident.

Able-bodied men and women were shipped to Germany for forced labor. By the summer of 1942, more than a million Soviets had been enslaved. Other slave laborers came from the ranks of the 5.7 million Soviet prisoners of war, the largest single group of Nazi victims other than the Jews.

In Berlin, SS bureaucrats drew up General Plan East, a blueprint for repopulating, with Germans, the lands that were being stripped of their native inhabitants. This resettlement phase would span several generations and military strongpoints would protect the German enclaves against any hostile natives. A few Slavs would be allowed to remain as a source of cheap labor; the rest would be driven east of the Urals into Siberia and central Asia.

The resettlement plan was shelved until the war with Russia was over, but the brutal killings went on. In the Ukraine alone, as many as four million noncombatants, including nearly a million Jews, were killed. More than half of Kiev's prewar population of 900,000 perished; between 150,000 and 200,000 were killed at Babi Yar. Countless others starved to death or were

*Janusz Korczak, whose real name was Henryk Goldszmit, was a physician, a writer, a radio personality, and Poland's most famous children's advocate. Most important in his life was an orphanage he directed, in which he put his educational methods to the test. When the Germans occupied Warsaw, Korczak was forced to move the orphanage into the ghetto where he then used all his connections and energy to help his orphans survive in dignity. He resisted the efforts of friends to escape the ghetto and seek safety. He would not leave without his children. In August 1942, the Nazis struck against the children's institutions in the ghetto. When he was ordered to surrender the orphans for deportation, Korczak marked them in rows of four, the children clutching flasks of water and their favorite books and toys. They marched through the ghetto to the plaza, where they joined thousands of others waiting to be put on trains. Korczak was with his children to the end. All were gassed at Treblinka.*

*During the uprising in the Warsaw ghetto, SS troops move in to attack a pocket of resistance. The Jewish fighters soon learned that partisan tactics were more effective and less costly than street fighting. They hid in dark hallways, striking quickly then escaping across rooftops. German troops moved cautiously and would not go down to cellars. Police dogs were used to uncover shelters where the fighters were hiding. Finally the SS commander ordered the ghetto burned, street by street, building by building.*

deported to Germany as slave labor, never to return. In Belorussia, an estimated 2.3 million civilians, one in four in the population, were killed; 200 towns and 9,000 villages were destroyed. When the war was over, an estimated 13 million Eastern Europeans had been sacrificed to Nazi racism.

The final death toll in Poland would reach six million, about 22 percent of the population. Half the victims were Jews. More than 2,600 Catholic priests were slain. Dead were more than half of the country's educated classes, including 45 percent of its physicians, 57 percent of its attorneys, 40 percent of its professors, and nearly 100 percent of its journalists.

In the summer of 1942, some 300,000 Jews were shipped from Warsaw to Treblinka, leaving only 60,000 in the ghetto. The remaining Jews became determined to resist. A new group was formed, *Zydowska Organizacja Bojowa* (ZOB), the Jewish Fighting Organization, and it slowly took control of the ghetto.

The ZOB issued a proclamation which read: "Jewish masses, the hour is drawing near. You must be prepared to resist. Not a single Jew should go to

*Ukrainian auxiliaries, fighting along with the SS to quell the Warsaw ghetto uprising, check their victims for signs of life. At the end, Jewish fighters hid in the sewers, even though the Germans tried first to flood then to smoke them out with smoke bombs. Resistance leader Mordecai Anielewicz wrote to one of his commanders: "What we have experienced cannot be described in words. We are aware of one thing only: what has happened has exceeded our dreams. The Germans ran twice from the ghetto . . . I have the feeling that great things are happening, that what we have dared is of great importance."*

the railroad cars. Those who are unable to put up active resistance should resist passively, should go into hiding . . . Our slogan must be: All are ready to die as human beings."

On April 19, 1943, Heinrich Himmler launched an operation to annihilate the Warsaw ghetto. The date was chosen because Hitler would be fifty-four years old on the following day, and the SS chief wanted to close another chapter in the Final Solution as a birthday gift for his Führer. Early on the 19th, a column of SS troops, supported by armored cars and small tanks rolled into the ghetto to round up the Jews who still lived there.

A band of Jewish guerrillas spoiled Himmler's birthday surprise. They ambushed the SS phalanx, firing small arms and hurling homemade grenades and Molotov cocktails from alleys, doorways and rooftops. Six hours later the stunned Germans withdrew. They returned the next day with 2,000 troops, but Jewish resistance was fierce, and what was planned as a three-day roundup became a bitter month-long campaign.

Outnumbered three-to-one, the untrained ghetto fighters knew they were doomed to fail, but they were determined to make the Nazis pay dearly for every inch of ground. One of the survivors, Alexander Donat, wrote that the uprising was undertaken "solely for death with dignity, and without the slightest hope of victory in life."

SS General Jürgen Stroop, facing a fight for control of every building, ordered his troops to burn the ghetto to the ground. He explained that it

*Observing the fighting in the Warsaw ghetto is SS Major General Juergen Stroop (wearing a cloth field cap), who commanded the German assault and would later be SS chief in Greece. His report to Himmler, "The Jewish quarter of Warsaw is no more!" was submitted as evidence before the International Military Tribunal in Nuremberg in 1946 and before the District Court of Warsaw in 1951, where he was sentenced to death and hanged.*

was the "only and ultimate way to defeat the rabble and scum of the earth and bring them above ground." Moving methodically from house to house, German engineers drenched wooden floors and staircases with gasoline, then watched the flames consume the neighborhood.

"The ghetto became a great blazing furnace, with no fresh air and suffocating heat and fetid odors," recalled a survivor. "The hiss of fire and the collapsing of buildings drowned out the sounds of gunfire, although from time to time the wind carried a human moan or distant scream."

With the homes aflame, thousands of Jews moved into makeshift bunkers, subterranean passageways, and sewers in order to evade capture. One partisan described two days in a sewer with water up to his lips: "Thirst was the worst handicap. Some even drank the thick, slimy sewer water. Every second seemed like months."

When Stroop and his men attempted to flood the sewer system, the Jews thwarted them by blowing up the control valves. The German troops then tossed smoke bombs and poisonous gas grenades into the underground labyrinth to kill those hiding there. Trained dogs were employed to sniff out other bunker dwellers.

Not until May 16th did General Stroop announce that the insurrection was over. "The Jewish Quarter of Warsaw is no more!" he reported to his superiors. It had taken the SS four weeks to clear a neighborhood that measured only 1,000 by 300 yards. To note the end of this "grand operation," Stroop blew up Warsaw's Grand Synagogue, an architectural treasure that stood outside the ghetto walls. He reported his losses at sixteen dead and 85 wounded, a gross understatement.

The uprising in the Warsaw ghetto was a revolution in Jewish history. Jews had met the Nazis with armed force. The significance of the event went far beyond the numbers who fought and died. On April 23, the ZOB commander, twenty-four-year old Mordecai Anielewicz, wrote to one of his unit commanders:

"What we have experienced cannot be described in words. We are aware of one thing only: what has happened has exceeded our dreams. The Germans ran twice from the ghetto . . . . I have the feeling that great things are happening, that what we have done is of great importance . . . ."

Most of the survivors would later die in concentration camps. Of the original 750 armed insurgents, fewer than a hundred managed to escape. The revolt of the Warsaw Ghetto demanded a change in German military responses to both deportations and subsequent ghetto liquidations. The Nazis similarly obliterated all the other ghettos in occupied Poland before they were driven out of the country by the Red Army.

# Chapter 9

*I stand in a cage before a hungry and angry tiger.*
*I stuff his mouth with meat, the flesh of my brothers*
*and sisters, to keep him in his cage lest*
*he break loose and tear us all to bits.*

## Moses Merin
### Chief of the Jewish councils in Upper Silesia

Reinhard Heydrich prided himself on being good at his job. So good, in fact, that he was marked for assassination. He arrived in Prague early in the fall of 1941 as the newly appointed Reich Protector for Bohemia and Monrovia, a position that gave him complete control over occupied Czechoslovakia. He made his headquarters at Hradcany Castle, once the home of Bohemian royalty.

"My task," he announced, "is to teach the Czech people that they cannot deny the reality of the relationship with the Reich, nor avoid the obedience that the Reich demands." Within two months, he had arrested 4,000 people and executed 400 of them.

Heydrich, the designer of Hitler's concentration-camp system, considered the appointment to be an advancement in his career. He consolidated his authority by retaining leadership of the powerful Reich Central Security Office and the *Einsatzgruppen* in the East. He would shuttle between Prague and Berlin to continue his role in preparing for the Final Solution.

One of his first tasks was to draw up plans to use Czech resources to bolster the Nazi offensive against Russia. In an early speech Heydrich announced: "I need calm in the region so that the Czech worker will perform to the best of his ability for the German war machine."

To enforce economic discipline, Heydrich used the stick and the carrot. Political offenders were shot, but economic criminals—hoarders and black marketeers—were publicly hanged. Among the first 400 he had killed, butchers outnumbered intellectuals, and profiteers outnumbered former Czech

Gas chambers were installed in two large concentration camps in the spring of 1942, Majdanek in Eastern Poland, shown here, and Auschwitz in Upper Silesia. Majdanek, located in a suburb of Lublin, received nearly a half million people, of whom 360,000— more than half of them Polish Jews— would die from starvation, exhaustion, disease and beatings. Seven gas chambers were employed, as were the camp's two wooden gallows. Die Endlosung, the Final Solution, was the extermination of Europe's Jews, and it became German policy on July 31, 1942. Majdanek and other Polish death camps received victims from all of occupied Europe—from Norway to Rumania. The liberators of Majdanek found a storehouse containing hundreds of thousands of shoes collected by the Nazis from their victims. They had been saved in the hope that a process would be developed to turn shoe leather to some practical or even military purpose.

military officers. At the same time, he encouraged work production by increasing food rations and pensions for industrial workers.

Heydrich spurned the armed security that the other Nazi officials insisted on. "Why should my Czechs shoot at me?" he said. But his daily commute from his villa fifteen miles south of the city was noted by two British-trained agents, Joseph Gabcik and Jan Kubis, who had parachuted into their homeland in December 1941.

After months of scouting and observing, the agents planned to assassinate Heydrich on the morning of May 27, 1942. Posting a lookout to signal the approach of Heydrich's Mercedes-Benz, they waited at a streetcar stop. Gabcik had a raincoat draped over a submachine gun. and Kubis carried grenades in a briefcase.

At 10:30 a.m. Heydrich rode by. He caught a glimpse of Gabcik pointing the submachine gun at him, but the weapon jammed. Kubis managed to toss a grenade that exploded under the right rear wheel of the car. As onlookers screamed, Heydrich staggered out of the disabled vehicle, drew his pistol and fired at the fleeing agents. Within minutes, however, he collapsed in the street. His driver gave chase but the agents escaped.

Learning of the attack, Hitler angrily exclaimed, "After what Heydrich has done for these Czechs!" He declared a state of siege in Czechoslovakia, offered a reward of a million marks for the capture of the assassins and vowed to slaughter 10,000 Czechs in reprisal.

In Prague's Bullock Hospital, Heydrich lay for a week with a broken rib, a pierced diaphragm, and a grenade splinter that jutted into his spleen. He insisted on being treated by German doctors. The prognosis for his recovery was optimistic, but suddenly, on June 4, he died of blood poisoning.

At an elaborate state funeral in Berlin, Himmler spoke glowingly of his former protégé. He called Heydrich an "ideal always to be emulated, but perhaps never again to be achieved." Hitler posthumously awarded Heydrich the German Order, the Reich's most distinguished medal. The Führer whispered to aides that Heydrich was "a man with a heart of iron."

On June 10, 1942, Germans came to Lidice, a village near Prague, in search of reprisal. The SS collected women and children for shipment to concentration camps, then lined up the men in groups of ten and shot them. Impatient with the pace of the killing, the SS commander forced the remaining men into a barn and set it ablaze. The Germans then torched the rest of the village.

The official German report stated that 192 adult males were shot, along with 71 women. The remaining 198 women and 98 children were deported to the Ravensbrück concentration camp. Only 143 women and 16 children returned to Lidice after the war. The Germans also reported removing 84,000 square yards of rubble from the razed village, which they then plowed over and planted with grain to remove any trace of habitation. Lidice ceased to exist.

Three weeks after Heydrich was ambushed, SS investigators had made no progress in finding the assassins. After moving between safe houses, they hid with several confederates in the crypt of the Church of Saint Cyril and Saint Methodius Church in Prague. Then Karel Curda, a Czech parachutist who had trained in Britain with the assassins, switched loyalties and betrayed their hideout to the SS.

As dawn broke on June 18, nineteen SS officers and 740 troops surrounded the church and opened fire, mortally wounding three of the agents. The SS demanded surrender, but the four survivors replied, "We are Czechs; we shall never surrender!" The SS tossed tear-gas canisters and pumped water into the crypt with no success. Finally, they dynamited open a huge slab covering a second entrance to the crypt. The two-hour siege ended when the Germans entered and found four wet and bloody bodies. The men who killed Heydrich had used their last bullets on themselves.

In tribute to the slain Reinhard Heydrich, his SS associates were preparing a new phase in the Final Solution. Code-named Operation Reinhard in his honor, it would be the logical follow-up to the massive round of killing carried out by the *Einsatzgruppen*. It called for the systematic extermination by gas poisoning of the estimated two million Jews concentrated in the ghettos of Poland. The operation was already underway at two new Polish camps, Belzec and Sobibor, and soon would be launched at a new camp at Treblinka.

Belzec, Sobibor and Treblinka were a kind of camp wholly new in human history. They were killing centers, pure and simple. Each existed solely for the purpose of murdering people as rapidly and efficiently as possible. No one was intended to survive. Men, women and children arrived by the trainload and were swept up in what an SS physician described as a *Laufenden Band* (conveyor belt). They were stripped of their clothing and their possessions, fed into the gas chambers and hauled away for burning or burial in less than three hours from arrival. The three camps could produce more than 25,000 deaths a day.

Gas chambers had been installed at two large camps—Majdanek in eastern Poland and Auschwitz in Upper Silesia. Auschwitz, as it turned out, would exterminate so many Jews that it became synonymous with the word Holocaust. But both of these camps maintained satellite labor camps which offered at least the faint possibility that inmates might work and survive.

These murder factories existed to fulfill Hitler's extreme anti-Semitic rhetoric. No written Hitler directives for the Final Solution were found after

*The interior of a Majdanek gas chamber. The stains on the wall are a chemical remnant of Zyklon B. Rudolf Höss, the commandant of Auschwitz, later described the killing process. "In the undressing room, prisoners (would be told) that they were going to be bathed and deloused, that they must leave the clothes neatly together . . . so that they would be able to find them again after delousing. The women went in first with their children, followed by the men . . . The door would now be quickly screwed up and the gas immediately discharged by waiting disinfectors through vents in the ceilings of the gas chamber down a shaft that led to the floor. . . It can be said that about one third died straight away. The remainder staggered and began to scream and struggle for air. The screaming soon changed to the death rattle and in a few minutes all lay still. After 20 minutes at the latest no movement could be discerned."*

the war, and it is likely he issued his orders orally. Himmler and Göring passed on the orders to subordinates, and the Wannsee conference confirmed the details. The Government General of Poland was given top priority in the implementation of the Final Solution. More than one-third of Europe's Jews lived there; it had a good railroad system; and the Germans believed that many Poles, given their history of anti-Semitism, would look the other way.

Himmler put Odilo Globocnik, the SS chief for the Lublin district in eastern Poland, in charge of Operation Reinhard. Nearly a hundred men who had become experts in operating gas chambers during the T-4 euthanasia program where assigned to Globocnik. Christian Wirth, who had conducted the first gassing experiments on the incurably insane, launched a pilot killing program in Warthegau in western Poland. He set up shop at the village of Chelmno, forty miles northwest of the Lodz ghetto, installed several motor vans that could accommodate up to 150 victims, and began to kill Jews.

There were problems at Chelmno. The carbon-monoxide exhaust from the vans simply didn't kill quickly enough, allowing for only about a thousand victims a day. Even still, the primitive facilities would eventually claim the lives of more than 200,000 Jews and several thousand Gypsies. Wirth believed that to handle the numbers projected for Operation Reinhard, stationary gas chambers would be necessary.

In early 1942, Wirth put his ideas into the design of Belzec, the prototype of the three death camps. It lay in a remote pine forest some 150 miles north of Warsaw. A rail line linked it to the big Jewish ghetto at Lublin, 75 miles to the north. Because Belzec was only meant to take lives, the premises were compact: 162 acres enclosed by barbed wire. In the compound was a small building containing three rooms disguised as shower baths. Carbon monoxide was produced by a diesel engine installed in a shed behind the gas chambers.

Belzec opened on March 17, 1942, with a trainload from the Lublin ghetto. The other two camps were modeled after Belzec but were slightly larger. Sobibor, about a hundred miles to the north, opened in May. The largest camp, Treblinka, seventy-five miles northeast of Warsaw, opened in late July. Wirth was made the supervisor and inspector of the three camps, and he was so brutal that even his subordinates referred to him as Christian the Terrible.

The camp commanders were all veterans of the euthanasia program. Each camp had a main staff of about thirty SS men who had sworn an oath of secrecy. The guards were a hundred or so Ukrainian prisoners of war, who volunteered for service as *Hilfswillige*, or German auxiliaries, equipped with rifles and whips.

The three camps were in full operation by the summer of 1942, and were receiving victims from all parts of the Reich's vastly expanded domain, which

*Deportation of Jews, Drohobycz, Poland 1942.*

stretched in a semicircular arc from Norway in the north around through Western Europe and into Rumania.

The Nazis went to great lengths to deceive the Jews coming from the western countries. To prevent panic and escape attempts, everyone was told that the deportees were bound for labor camps or farms in the East. Some of the trains were made up of ordinary passenger coaches instead of freight cars, which heightened the illusion of a peaceful journey to "resettlement in the East."

Less deception was needed in the ghettos of Poland. The deportees were told they would be resettled in the Ukraine. Typically, they were given less than a day's notice. Deportation authorities used pressure to gain the cooperation of Jewish leaders. When they approached Moses Merin, chief of the Jewish councils in Upper Silesia, he agreed to help, in the desperate but mistaken belief that the sacrifice of some of his people would save the majority. Two years later he would say: "I stand in a cage before a hungry and angry tiger. I stuff his mouth with meat, the flesh of my brothers and sisters, to keep him in his cage lest he break loose and tear us all to bits."

Not all Jewish leaders cooperated. Adam Czerniakow, chairman of the Jewish Council in the Warsaw ghetto, was ordered to supply 6,000 Jews to fill the first trains to Treblinka. He was told that if he failed, his wife would be taken hostage and shot. Faced with an impossible choice, Czerniakow committed suicide.

At first many Polish Jews went willingly to the trains. Some 20,000 in Warsaw volunteered for relocation in return for a special ration of bread and jam. Many went in desperation, hoping for a better life in a labor camp.

After word of the death camps spread, ghetto inhabitants began to resist and indiscriminate cruelty marked the ghetto roundups. Anyone who resisted or attempted to elude arrest was shot down, as were many others who were deemed too old, too sick or too young. Husbands and wives were separated. Mothers were snatched from their babies and taken away. No one was safe in the roundups. "He who walked too quickly was shot," a survivor later recounted. "He who fell on the way was shot. He who strayed out of line was shot. He who turned his head was shot. He who bent down was shot. He who spoke too loudly was shot. A child who cried was shot."

Jews traveled to the death camps without food, water or toilets. The cars were bolted shut and boarded up to prevent escape. They reeked with the stench of excrement and the quicklime strewn on the floor as a disinfectant. Desperate mothers gave children urine to quiet their thirst. Long delays en route increased the suffering. On a typical day, trains carrying as many as 25,000 Jews made their way to the camps. Their progress was impeded by track shutdowns, poor planning and bottlenecks at the camp. Treblinka, for instance, was not prepared to receive trains after dark.

As the trains waited, the horror increased. In search of water for their dying children, mothers thrust empty bottles fastened to sticks through openings in the car walls and threw out money and gold rings and other jewelry. The guards smashed the bottles, pocketed the money and jewelry, and shot those who begged for water and anyone who tried to give it to them.

Thousands died on the way to the camps. They died of suffocation and dehydration, took their own lives, or were trampled to death in the cars. The guards who lay atop the cars or perched on the bumpers at either end of a car shot at those passengers who tried to escape. Poles who lived near the death camps would remember that the sounds of rifle fire usually signaled the approach of a trainload of Jews.

# Chapter 10

*I rarely saw them as individuals.*
*It was always a huge mass.*

**Franz Stangl**
**Treblinka commandant**

From the moment the train arrived, every step in the extermination process was carefully orchestrated. The goal was to kill all but a few selected Jews within two hours. To accomplish this, Christian Wirth developed at Belzec a prescription involving deception, speed and dehumanization, which was later applied to the other camps.

For Jews coming from Western Europe, the Germans preserved the illusion of a peaceful journey to a new home. At Treblinka, they created a false train station to suggest that it was only a transit camp, a stopover on the way to better things. Signs indicated such nonexistent amenities as a restaurant, ticket office and telephone. At Sobibor, Jewish inmates helped the new arrivals with their luggage and gave them false checks for reclaiming it. The Germans even passed out postcards and asked the Jews to write home to report their safe arrival.

When the train stopped, Jewish inmates unbolted the doors, then dragged away the corpses littering the cars. SS men and Ukrainian guards hurried the others on with whips, rifles and incessant shouting. "Everything was done at lightning speed," a survivor recalled. "We had no time to think."

This brutal show of force had a purpose. It was designed by Wirth to deter resistance or escape by paralyzing the victims' reactions and preventing them from realizing what was going on. It also increased the daily productivity of the camp. By treating arrivals like livestock, it made it easier for the guards to do their job.

Camp officials classified the new arrivals. A few craftsmen and the strongest young people were sent to the camp work force. Then the guards weeded out those who could not keep up—the elderly, invalids, babies and toddlers. These unfortunates were taken away by Jewish workers to a special

*The railroad station at Treblinka, the death camp about fifty miles north of Warsaw where some 300,000 Jews from the Warsaw ghetto were exterminated. It also was the only death camp that had a major revolt by prisoners. The guards forced some inmates to become what the Germans called* Totenjuden, *Jews of Death. They removed the bodies from the gas chambers and removed gold teeth from the victims. Although scorned by the condemned, the Jews of Death knew they held the testimony of Treblinka and could give it if some escaped. They started a revolt on August 3, 1943, killing about twenty guards with weapons taken from an armory opened with keys fashioned by an inmate locksmith. About 600 of the thousand who escaped managed to reach the nearby forest. When the Soviet army arrived a year later, they found only forty former prisoners still alive.*

killing area. At Treblinka it was called the *Lazarett,* or infirmary. The attendants wore Red Cross armbands. The executioner, SS Sergeant August Miete, known to prisoners as the Angel of Death, dispatched them with a pistol shot to the nape of the neck. The victims fell into an open pit, where bodies were constantly being burned.

For the others, the welcoming speech was the final stage in the arrival process. They were reassured that this was a transit camp, that they would undergo disinfection in the baths to prevent the spread of disease, and then be sent on to work in the Ukraine. To prepare them for the "baths," the

Germans separated the men from the women and children, herded them into barracks and ordered them to strip. The women had their hair cut close to the scalp.

The passageway to the gas chambers was known to the staff as "The Tube," or "The Road to Heaven." At Treblinka, it was a road about fifteen feet wide bordered by seven-foot-high barbed wire entwined with branches so no one could see in or out. The SS men forced the nude victims to run its 110-yard length, urged on by whips and clubs. Men went first because the overseers feared they would resist if they saw what was happening to the women. At last the victims stood, waiting their turn, in front of the building with the sign "Baths and Inhalation Rooms." By then they must have suspected what awaited them.

The entrance to the bath house at Treblinka was flanked by pots of geraniums. A large Star of David adorned the front gable, and the entrance was covered with a heavy dark curtain. It had been taken from a synagogue and still bore the Hebrew legend, "This is the gate through which the righteous shall enter."

The Jews were pushed and shoved into the tiled chambers with their fake shower nozzles. Some prayed, some cursed. Sometimes they were told to raise their arms and pull in their stomachs so that more people could be squeezed in. When the chamber could hold no more, the heavy wooden door was slammed shut.

"Ivan, water!" was the signal to start the diesel engine that would pump carbon monoxide into the chamber. Sometimes the engine would fail to start, and victims stood for hours in agony inside the chamber. Others waited outside, sometimes in cold so fierce that their naked feet froze to the ground.

Sooner or later the engine would start and fumes would pour into the chamber. Cries and moans rose, then subsided. Then, recalled Rudolf Reder, one of only two Jews to survive Belzec, "came one last terrible shout." A guard would listen at the wall or look through a small glass peephole to see if there were any signs of life. The all-clear signal was usually given about thirty minutes after the engine was switched on. The guards would open the door, and the Jewish inmates of the so-called death brigade began the ghastly task of clearing the gas chambers.

"The people were still standing like columns of stone, with no room to fall or lean," recalled SS Lieutenant Kurt Gerstein, who had visited Belzec. "Even in death you could tell the families, all holding hands. It was difficult to separate them while emptying the room for the next batch. The bodies were tossed out, blue, wet with sweat and urine, the legs smeared with excrement and menstrual blood. Two dozen workers were busy checking mouths, which they opened with iron hooks. Dentists knocked out gold teeth, bridges and crowns with hammers."

In the early days, the bodies were buried. Driven by their overseers, the death-brigade Jews dragged or carried the bodies to enormous ditches. The burial process soon proved inadequate. Jews were being killed faster than they could be put in the ground. Meanwhile, Heinrich Himmler was searching for a better way to cover up the evidence of the final solution. A small group, using the code name *Aktion* 1005 (Special Command 1005), briefly experimented with incendiary bombs but finally settled on cremation over enormous open fireplaces. Any bones that remained after burning were reduced in a special bone-crushing device. Ashes and bone fragments were then buried in the pits from which the bodies had been disinterred.

Treblinka's burning operations were documented by eyewitnesses. Some 700,000 corpses were unearthed and cremated, while bodies fresh from the gas chambers were being disposed of. Mechanical excavators dug up the corpses, six or eight to the scoop, and dumped them on the ground. Teams of Jewish prisoners then transferred them on stretchers to gigantic steel grids that could hold as many as 3,000 stacked-up bodies. The 100-foot-wide grid consisted of a half-dozen railroad rails, resting on three rows of twenty-eight-inch-high concrete posts.

At first, the bodies were doused with gasoline, but the SS men made a discovery—women burned more rapidly then men because their bodies pos-

*Prisoners toil at Mauthausen, in Austria, the last camp to be liberated by the Americans. In its final four months of operation, more than 30,000 people had been slain here, or had died from starvation and disease. All inmates at Mauthausen—Jews, Gypsies, homosexuals, religious prisoners, Russians and Spaniards— were subject to the same vicious cruelties. A British officer imprisoned here described how he "became familiar with the gas lorries and the sight of prisoners loaded into them who died on the way to nowhere." American broadcast correspondent Fred Friendly remembers Mauthausen: "Of all the sights and sounds that stunned me, the weakness of the brave men and women who survived was the most memorable. . . When we walked through (the barracks), they shouted in various languages, 'Viva, Americanski.' But their hands were so emaciated, so much without flesh, that it sounded to me . . . like seals clapping."*

sessed more fat. If female bodies were arranged in the bottom layer, gasoline was unnecessary. The smell of flesh burning at the rate 7,000 bodies a day could be detected for miles around.

The gas chambers at Treblinka each measured twelve by twenty-seven feet. The ceilings were low to shorten asphyxiation time and save on carbon monoxide. The Treblinka commandant, Franz Stangl, testified after the war that the camp could liquidate a thousand people an hour. "When the work lasted for about fourteen hours," he said, "12,000 to 15,000 people were annihilated. There were many days that the work lasted from the early morning until the evening."

While teams of inmates reduced the bones to particles, others processed the plunder taken from the victims. Clothing, jewelry, money, watches, eyeglasses, baby carriages, bedding, briefcases and other belongings had to be cleaned and sorted. Currency, dental gold and other articles of high value went to the German central bank. Other items were sold or distributed to SS men and their families. By official accounting, more than $70 million in money and goods was confiscated from Jews at Belzec, Sobibor and Treblinka.

The so-called work Jews who were chosen for work details rather than for the gas chamber did all the physical labor and enabled the camp to function. At first they would be killed after a day or two, but this proved inefficient. Camp administrators created semi-permanent work forces for as many as a thousand inmates.

Some were specialists: the *Friseurs* cut hair, the *Goldjuden*, or gold Jews, sorted out the valuables, including the gold extracted by the dentists. Tailors, carpenters, shoemakers and other craftsmen were called "Court Jews" because the German staff relied on them for personal services. At Treblinka, the teams assigned to the various steps in the killing cycle were organized so efficiently that they had their own color-coded armbands or badges. Each group was supervised by a Jewish *Kapo* (from the Italian *capo*, for chief), usually chosen by the Germans for his willingness to punish his own people.

A work Jew rarely survived more than a few months. Food usually consisted of a watery turnip soup, sawdust bread and whatever the inmates could pilfer from packages carried by victims on the trains. Dysentery, typhus and skin diseases were epidemic. Prisoners were often flogged, and sometimes shot. Roll calls were dreaded; the Germans used them to weed out anyone with signs of sickness or weakness. Those selected were liquidated and replaced with new arrivals.

"The selection was a constant threat, like a drawn sword over our heads," wrote Abraham Kszepicki, a work Jew who escaped from Treblinka. "In the morning, we would awaken before the signal and arrange our appearance to look better. Never, in the best of times, did we shave so often as in Treblinka. Every morning, everyone would shave and wash his face in eau de cologne taken from the bundles left by [dead] Jews. Some powdered their faces and even rouged their lips, pinched their cheeks till they were rosy, and all this to gain another few days of life, perhaps a few weeks, who knew?"

The SS men who ran the camps were a strange lot. A few were remembered for small kindnesses, such as providing extra food. Others were simply brutes. A former inmate at Sobibor, remembers the pastime of one guard:

*Map of Treblinka showing train station (Bahnhof), barracks (Baracke), and gas chambers (Gaskammern).*

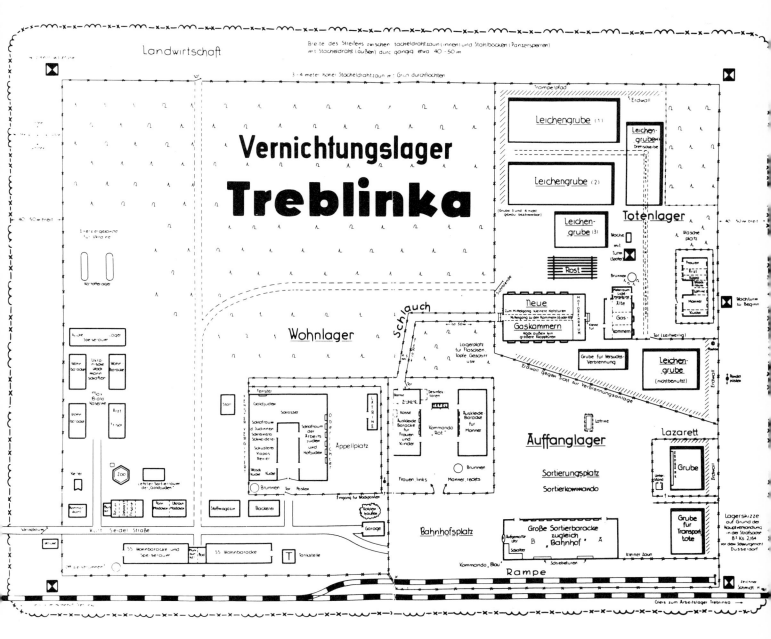

"On his way to lunch he was in the habit of passing by the main gate and swinging a whip with all his strength upon the heads of the Jews who went through—this to increase his appetite for the meal that awaited him."

Franz Stangl, the second commander of Treblinka, was an Austrian who had been a master weaver before becoming a police investigator and then joining the Nazi euthanasia program. He was a devoted family man, a Catholic, and did not seem sadistic by temperament. He had little contact with his victims, although he met the train dressed in impeccable white linen riding clothes. He later said he regarded the victims as inhuman cargo: "I rarely saw them as individuals. It was always a huge mass." He seemed to have taken pride in overseeing the death camp, although he drank brandy every night to help him sleep.

In contrast, Kurt Franz, his second-in-command, was described as a "sadist of exquisite cruelty." A veteran of the euthanasia program and Buchenwald, he was a former boxer who liked to use inmates as punching bags. He also enjoyed throwing babies against a wall. He had a large dog, Barry, whom he trained to attack the genitals of his victims.

The SS overseers encouraged entertainment among the work Jews. They allowed chess and card games, promoted love affairs and even staged mock marriages between inmates. At Belzec there were Sunday soccer games between the staff and the work Jews. Every camp had a small musical ensemble to entertain the staff and to help drown out the tumult of the killings.

The most ambitious orchestra was at Treblinka, where the director, Artur Gold, a prominent conductor in Warsaw before the war, had been plucked naked from the gas chamber procession. Dressed in special blue and white suits, Gold's ten-man group performed at special events. They also played at evening roll call, which ended with the inmates singing the Treblinka anthem, a hymn to "work, obedience and duty."

The Nazis believed that these diversions would keep the inmates from thinking about resistance or escape. Camp commandants required passive victims to keep the operation running smoothly. But things began happening that made them uneasy. Himmler had ordered the liquidation of all the Jews in the Government Central in Poland by the end of 1942, and that had nearly been done. Belzec had shut down its gas chambers, and the pace of killing at the other camps had slowed. The commandants feared what would happen when the work Jews realized that their days were numbered.

# Chapter 11

## *All right, give them something nice to chew on.*

## At Birkenau, the signal to drop the canisters of Zyklon B

In September 1942, Meir Berliner, a work Jew at Treblinka, stepped out of line at evening roll call and plunged a homemade knife into the back of an SS guard, mortally wounding him. Berliner and more than 150 of his fellow work Jews were shot in reprisal. Two months later, youths arriving at Treblinka from the Bialystok area chose not to submit passively. One tossed a grenade, and others attacked the Germans and Ukrainians with knives and fists. Their revolt was short-lived. All the youths were shot or gassed.

In the death camps, resistance began as isolated acts of desperation. Work Jews, individually or in small groups, attempted to escape. They managed to climb over a fence at night, or hide in stacks of clothing being shipped out in freight cars. After word of the true fate of deportees reached the ghettos, thousands of Jews either attempted to elude the roundups or jumped from the trains taking them to the death camps.

Only a few of those who escaped the Polish camps made it to freedom. Most of the Poles they encountered were either indifferent or hostile. The Poles knew that the Germans would kill them if they helped Jews and reward them if they betrayed the Jews. The fugitives felt insecure in the countryside and tended to go back to the ghetto but found they faced the same problem all over again when they were caught in another deportation.

By the time news of the uprising in the Warsaw ghetto reached Treblinka in May 1943, the work Jews there had already formed their own resistance group. The members organized themselves into teams, chose their leaders and accepted special assignments for the day of the planned uprising. A locksmith had made a key to the camp arsenal, and rifles and grenades would be taken and quietly distributed to the teams from a handcart. Then the worker responsible for the daily decontamination of the camp would use gasoline

*Acts of rebellion could be personal as with suicide, or collective, as with revolts at Treblinka and Sobibor. Here an inmate at Mauthausen has elected to determine his own fate.*

*Rosa Robota was a Jewish underground activist in Auschwitz. On October 7, 1944, the* Sonderkommando *blew up one of Birkenau's four crematoria. An elaborate underground network smuggled dynamite to the* Sonderkommando. *The explosion was followed by the mass escape of 600 prisoners. Rosa Robota and three other women accused of supplying the dynamite were hanged in the presence of the remaining inmates. As the trapdoor was opened Roza shouted, "Hazak v'ematz!" (Be strong, have courage!).*

rather than disinfectant in order to prepare the wooden buildings for the torch. The revolt was repeatedly delayed. The plotters knew their days were numbered as they saw fewer and fewer trains arriving at the camp. Zero hour was finally set for 4:30 p.m, August 2, 1943. The appointed day was hot and sultry. The camp commander was drinking with a friend in his quarters. His deputy had taken a group of twenty or so staff members to swim in the nearby Bug River. As the hour approached, an SS sergeant became suspicious and had to be shot. His suspicions forced a premature start which threw the revolt into turmoil. Not all the weapons had yet been distributed. However, the rebels wounded a German, killed or wounded a half-dozen Ukrainians and set many of the buildings on fire. Most of the 850 work Jews managed to break out of the camp.

The Germans sent in a full trainload of reinforcements to track down the fugitives, recapturing all but about a hundred. Kurt Franz oversaw the subsequent dismantling and destruction of the camp as Treblinka was then shut

*The crematoria of Auschwitz. The bodies of literally millions of men, women and children were stuffed into these ovens, three or four at a time, and reduced to ashes. Crematorium II had fifteen ovens, which could burn between forty-five and seventy-five corpses at once, and about a thousand people in one day. Alice Lok, a sixteen-year-old Hungarian Jew, managed to enter a gas chamber and survive. She described her experience: "One day they said to us, 'You will get winter clothes. Go. March up.' They selected a bunch of children. The Blockaltester [block supervisor] selected the children . . . I said to Edith, 'Don't worry. I will come back and bring you some warm clothes. I will just snitch another one extra for you.' They took us to a shower. They said it will be a disinfection first, but instead of a shower or a disinfection, it was a different place. There was a window, and on it was written Bathhouse. They took away our clothes. They asked us to put our clothes down, and we will get it back after the disinfection. But it turned out that the shower did not work, that it was really the gas. I know only that it was dark, that the Germans were terribly nervous, that when we came out they were very, very angry."*

down; it received its last trainload of deportees on August 19, only seventeen days after the revolt.

At Sobibor, a revolt committee debated for months but couldn't decide what they should do. The situation in the camp became urgent in June, 1943, when 600 work Jews, who had been burning old corpses at Belzec, were transferred to Sobibor and shot. The dwindling number of trains arriving at Sobibor indicated that a similar fate awaited its work Jews.

Over the summer, a number of abortive plots were hatched at Sobibor—poison the food of the staff, bribe the Ukrainian guards, set fire to the clothing warehouse, dig tunnels. The guards discovered one tunnel and shot 150 prisoners in reprisal.

The prisoners needed a leader and one arrived in late summer on a trainload of 2,000 Jews from Minsk. His name was Lieutenant Alexander Pechersky, and he was one of about a hundred men on the train who had been taken prisoner while serving in the Red Army. Pechersky had already attempted to escape from a prisoner-of-war camp, and was eager to try again. Within a week of his arrival, he was made chief of the underground and charged with organizing a mass escape.

The uprising was set for October 14, only three days after the last train of deportees would arrive at the camp. At the time of the uprising, a dozen or so SS men were on vacation, including the camp commander. Pechersky's plan called for getting rid of the remaining key staff members.

Beginning in mid-afternoon, SS officials were lured under various pretexts, one by one, to the tailor shop, shoemaker's, and other workshops. There inmates wielding axes attacked and killed them. By 5:00 p.m., eight SS men lay dead, telephone and electric wires had been cut, and the stove repairman had smuggled six rifles out of the Ukrainian guard barracks—all without alerting the remaining staff members.

Even more daring was the second phase of the plan. The 600 prisoners would assemble routinely for evening roll call as if nothing had happened, then march out of the main gate before the now-leaderless Ukrainian guards realized something was wrong. But a German noticed the pushing and jostling in the roll call ranks, intervened, and was struck down by hatchets. At this moment, Pechersky and his lieutenants lost control of the revolt.

The inmates tried to break into the armory for more weapons, but failed. Now under fire from the guards, they broke through the fences and into the lethal minefields beyond, clambering over the blown-up bodies of their comrades.

Sobibor was in total confusion, and it was morning before the Germans could mount a full-scale search. Of the 600 inmates, perhaps seventy survived the war, including Pechersky and a half-dozen or so of his fellow Red Army veterans who made their way across the Bug River and joined Soviet partisans operating in the area.

Earlier, Himmler had told a group of high-ranking officers: "This [Operation Reinhhard] is a page of glory in our history that has never been written and that is never to be written." Now there were scores of desperate fugitives from Treblinka and Sobibor who would live to bear witness.

Operation Reinhard was now officially over. Some 1.7 million people, all but a few of them Jews, had been annihilated in the three extermination camps during a period of nineteen months. The Jewish ghettos had been eliminated, and only a few Jews were still alive in the Government General.

Painstaking care was taken to erase every trace of the Polish death camps. Buildings were razed and plowed under; trees and grass were planted where they once stood. Ukrainians were paid to live there with their families. They guarded the premises from neighboring Poles who had already dug up the refurbished ground at Belzec looking for valuables. At Treblinka, the Ukrainian who lived there was a former guard, and his house was made of bricks taken from the dismantled gas chambers.

Treblinka, Sobibor and Belzec were gone but another camp would replace them. It was Auschwitz, and it would become the ultimate murder factory. It was located in a swampy area of Upper Silesia, a region annexed by Germany from the southwest corner of occupied Poland. It opened in June 1940, to serve as a penal camp for Polish political prisoners.

During the summer of 1941, the commandant of Auschwitz, Rudolf Höss, an SS captain, was summoned to Berlin by Heinrich Himmler and given a highly secret mission. Auschwitz, Himmler said, had been selected as a principal center for the extermination of the Jews. The moral implications of the assignment didn't seem to bother Höss, but he was concerned about the practical mechanics of murder on a grand scale.

Höss believed that the carbon-monoxide process used in the euthanasia program and later adopted by the early death camps was impractical for his new assignment. He began to look around for something more efficient. Secret orders had come down in September, 1941 to execute a group of Soviet prisoners transferred to Auschwitz from other camps. One of Höss's deputies tried an experiment.

The prisoners were crammed into a block of underground detention cells, then pellets of a substance called Zyklon B were thrown into the cells. Ordinarily used as an insecticide to fumigate barracks, Zyklon B consisted of crystals of prussic acid, a solid chemical that turns into highly lethal hydrogen cyanide gas when it comes into contact with air. The pellets unleashed their

*Zyklon B, the commercial name for prussic acid gas, was used in the gas chambers of Auschwitz, Birkenau and Majdanek to kill Jews in great numbers. Zyklon B was a common and highly poisonous insecticide, and ironically, concentration camps were using it to kill rats and insects before it was found to be ideal for killing humans. The gas was contained in chalky pellets. Those shown are from Majdanek. The canister is from Auschwitz. The SS used Zyklon B from September 1941 until January 1945.*

bitter, almond-like odor, and the Russians died within minutes, as did hundreds of other prisoners subjected to further experiments.

"Protected by a gas mask, I watched the killing myself," Höss later wrote. ". . . Death came the moment the Zyklon B was thrown in. A short, almost smothered cry, and it was all over." Zyklon B killed in half the time required by carbon monoxide. Höss would recall that he was "considerably excited by the efficiency of the experiment." It "set my mind to rest," he wrote. "Now we had the gas, and we had established a procedure."

Auschwitz differed from the earlier death camps of Operation Reinhard in ways other than this new technology of killing. It rapidly became one of

A group of women and children await the selection process at Auschwitz—a handful of the 434, 351 Hungarian Jews who were shipped here in 147 trains between May 15 and July 9, 1944. One survivor described what it felt like to arrive at Auschwitz: "The climax came suddenly. The door opened with a crash, and the dark echoed with outlandish orders in that curt, barbaric barking of Germans in command . . . A vast platform appeared before us, lit up by reflectors. A little beyond it, a row of lorries . . . A dozen SS men . . . began to interrogate us . . . 'How old? Healthy or ill?' And on the basis of the reply they pointed in one of two different directions."

the largest of the German concentration and extermination camps, comprising three main compounds and three dozen satellite camps sprawling over nearly twenty square miles, and housing a peak population of close to 160,000 inmates.

Trainloads of Jews came to Auschwitz from virtually every country occupied by Germany. They worked alongside other prisoners in vital war industries, enduring conditions so horrible and alien that inmates spoke of Auschwitz as "another planet." Most workers died within a few months, their bodies were disposed of in the up-to-date crematoriums Höss had built to go with his gas chambers.

As at Treblinka and its sister camps, death was Auschwitz's most important product. The major difference was that Auschwitz operated longer, killed more efficiently and claimed more victims. Through Zyklon B, shooting, hanging, torture, overwork, starvation and disease, at least one million Jews and a quarter of a million others died at Auschwitz.

The mass killings of Jews with Zyklon B began in the spring of 1942. The first killings at Auschwitz related to the Final Solution took place there on May 4,when some 1,200 Jews chosen from recent transports from Germany, Slovakia and France were gassed.

Commandant Höss soon decided that the first killing site was too exposed to the eyes of the inmates. He shifted activities to a new, more secluded camp he created about two miles west of the main installation at Auschwitz. The camp was situated in a forest and built around two old peasant cottages, charmingly whitewashed and topped with thatched roofs. The Germans blocked up most of the windows and added airtight interior walls and doors, subdividing each of the cottages (Bunkers No. 1 and No. 2 in camp terminology) into four gas chambers. The new killing center became known as Birkenau because of the lovely birch trees that shaded it.

The techniques of mass killing were constantly being refined by Höss and his SS staff. Höss became an arch rival of Christian Wirth, the chief executioner of Operation Reinhard. The two men refused to share ideas. Höss learned the hard way to have the victims disrobe before entering the gas chambers. The first Jews to be gassed at Auschwitz were fully dressed, and their clothing was so stained that none of it could be reclaimed for later use. Höss changed the procedure to have victims disrobe outside, then when he noted this caused the victims to be embarrassed and apprehensive, he built barracks nearby where men and women could disrobe in privacy.

"It was most important," he wrote, "that the whole business of arriving and undressing should take place in an atmosphere of greatest possible calm." To this end, he formed a string orchestra of female inmates, dressed them in

An aerial view of Auschwitz taken in August 1944, shows the main features of the infamous camp: the rows of prisoner barracks, the gas chamber and crematorium, the camp headquarters, even a row of new prisoners being registered. International Jewish leaders urged the British and Americans to initiate a bombing campaign to disrupt the rail traffic between Hungary and Auschwitz. The Allies refused, although the camp was within range of bombers based in southern Italy. Ironically, a month later bombs from American B-24s attacking nearby Monowitz fell short and destroyed a barracks at the Auschwitz main camp, killing fifteen SS men and injuring twenty-eight. A cluster of bombs also was mistakenly dropped at Birkenau, damaging the railroad but missing the crematoriums.

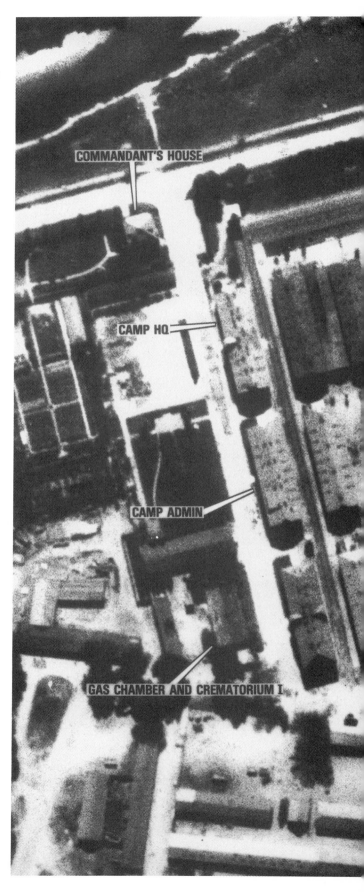

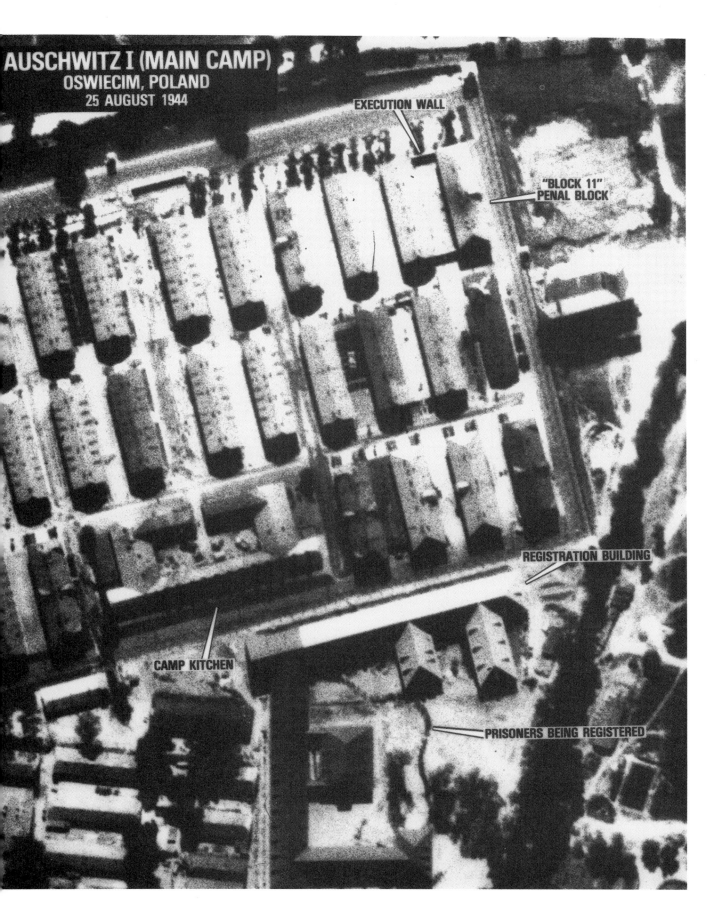

AUSCHWITZ I (MAIN CAMP)
OSWIECIM, POLAND
25 AUGUST 1944

EXECUTION WALL

"BLOCK 11"
PENAL BLOCK

REGISTRATION BUILDING

CAMP KITCHEN

PRISONERS BEING REGISTERED

white blouses and dark blue skirts, who played cheerful pieces as the train-loads of deportees arrived at Auschwitz, from which they marched or were trucked to Birkenau.

During the first year of operation at Birkenau, it became clear that the facilities were inadequate for killing on a massive scale. Himmler visited the camp and gave Höss his approval for an ambitious expansion plan. Crews of inmates began building a complex of four state-of-the-art killing centers. Each was a brick crematorium, combining under one roof all the necessary facilities for the complete extermination process, from undressing to gassing and cremation in specially designed furnaces.

The first of the new killing centers began operation in March, 1943. Prominent guests came from Berlin to witness the special inaugural program—the gassing and cremation of Jews from Krakow. The other crematoriums were completed during the next three months. The four killing

*Trains with freight cars jammed with Jewish men, women and children came down these tracks to the depot at Auschwitz. Before the sun set, most would be gassed and their bodies reduced to ashes in the crematorium. Those who lived had a variety of experiences. Some were political prisoners, others were slave laborers. Some worked as Sonderkommando, feeding bodies into the crematoria. All lived and worked in the shadow of death, and for some this became too much. They lost hope and gave up. They became* Musselmaner, *the walking dead.*

*Hungarian Jewish women—new arrivals at Auschwitz, their hair clipped to the scalp and wearing their new uniforms—are marched off to take part in the selection process. In a few minutes most will be marked for death. Fritzie Fritshall, a survivor, arrived at Auschwitz when she was only 15 years old. She later recalled: "How does one describe the walking into Auschwitz, the smell? And someone pointing out to you that those are gas chambers, that your parents went up in smoke. When I asked, 'When will I see my mother?' several hours after I came into the camp, I was shown the smoke. This is how I found out where she went."*

centers contained a total of six gas chambers and fourteen ovens for cremating up to 8,000 corpses a day. Deceptive with their steep roofs, dormer windows, stout chimneys and tasteful landscaping, these one-story red brick structures deliberately resembled modern German industrial buildings.

In the two largest complexes at Birkenau, the victims descended a flight of steps into underground facilities. Promising them baths, the SS executioners herded them into large anterooms, persuaded them to undress and to hang their clothing neatly on numbered hooks. The victims were then pushed into a chamber, the largest of which was more than 250 square yards in area. The chamber contained, in addition to imitation water taps and nozzles, a row of concrete pillars, interspersed with floor-to-ceiling columns with perforated metal sides.

The heavy steel door was bolted shut, and an ambulance with spurious Red Cross markings pulled up outside the crematoriums. Out jumped the so-called disinfectors—SS men wearing gas masks, carrying green tin canisters of Zyklon B. They went onto the grassy terrace that covered the chamber, lifted steel trapdoors concealed by mushroom-like concrete forms projecting above the terrace and knocked open the canisters.

Upon command—"All right, give them something nice to chew on."—the SS men poured the pea-sized pellets through the ducts into the perforated columns. The motors of the transport trucks were then revved up to drown out the "heartrending weeping, cries for help, fervent prayers, violent banging, and knocking," reported Filip Müller, who served for two-and-a-half years as a *Sonderkommando*, the special squad of inmates charged with body disposal.

The Zyklon B crystals rattled to the bottom of the columns and turned into hydrogen cyanide gas. The very young and the very old died before the others because the gas saturated the lower part of the room first. The stronger ones struggled to the top, clawing and trampling one another, and climbing over layers of bodies. But within a few minutes, the deadly gas filled the chamber.

When movement inside the chamber stopped, an SS physician, watching this macabre scene through a peephole in the door, gave the signal to switch on the ventilators that pumped the gas from the room, where it would dissipate harmlessly into the open air. Pockets of gas lingered amid the entangled layers of victims, and members of the Sonderkommando wore protective masks when they entered to hose down the dead and clear the chamber. They pried apart the intertwined corpses, removed gold teeth, and cut the women's hair. Then, using a leather strap looped around a body's wrist, they dragged the dead one at a time onto the elevator, which carried them up one story to the furnace room.

The furnace roared like an inferno. "The force and heat of the flames were so great that the whole room rumbled and trembled," Filip Müller would recall. There were as many as five ovens per chamber, most of which had three compartments each. Below the grate oven blazed a coke-fed fire. Pairs of inmates heaped two or three bodies onto a metal stretcher and lifted it onto rollers at the opening of a chamber. They pushed the stretcher in, held the corpses on the grate with a large metal fork, and pulled the stretcher out. Three bodies were consumed in about twenty minutes. Later, inmates with metal scrapers raked out the gray-white ashes from the bottom of the ovens. These last remains were trucked to one of the nearby rivers, the Vistula or the Sola, and dumped into the water.

To shorten the time needed to burn the corpses, a series of experiments were conducted in the autumn of 1943. Technicians from Topf and Sons, the

*The words over the entrance to Auschwitz promises that "Work shall make you free," but only death awaited prisoners sent here. Until 1941, the camp had only some 9,000 prisoners. But with the invasion of the Soviet Union it was expanded time and again until Rudolf Höss, the camp commandant, could boast that Auschwitz was "the greatest extermination center of all time." By his account, more than 2.5 million people were killed by mass execution or in gas chambers and another 500,000 starved to death. He complained that he "could dispose of 2,000 heads in a half hour, but it was the burning that took all the time."*

German firm that had manufactured and installed the furnaces, measured the combustibility of different types of coke and corpses. They concluded that the best oven load consisted of one well-nourished, fast-burning adult, one child, and one emaciated adult already reduced to skin and bone by starvation and labor. This combination of bodies, once it caught fire, would continue to burn without requiring further amounts of precious coke.

The system worked well. Trainload after trainload of Jews from the four corners of western Europe arrived and the occupants were reduced to ashes in a matter of hours. But once in a long while something would go wrong.

# Chapter 12

## *May I tell you a grim story?*

## SS Lieutenant Kurt Gerstein
### Procurement Officer for Zyklon B

An incident occurred on October 23, 1943, when some 1,700 Polish Jews arrived at Auschwitz from the Bergen-Belsen concentration camp in Germany. They had been repeatedly duped by the Nazis. Many had held visas to South American countries, and they had been lured out of hiding in Warsaw by promises of allowing them to emigrate. Then they paid large bribes to obtain exit permits. After being sent to Bergen-Belsen, they were moved to Auschwitz under the ruse that they were being taken to Switzerland and to freedom.

When they were taken to the killing complex at Birkenau, according to Filip Müller, more than half of them had already been pushed into the gas chamber when the rest, still in the changing room, grew suspicious and refused to undress. SS men moved in with sticks flailing.

Suddenly, Müller wrote, the two SS men "stopped in their tracks, attracted by a strikingly handsome woman with blue-black hair who was taking off her right shoe. The woman, as soon as she noticed that the SS men were ogling her, launched into what appeared to be a titillating and seductive striptease act. She had taken off her blouse and was standing in front of her lecherous audience in her brassiere. Then she steadied herself against a concrete pillar with her left arm and bent down, slightly lifting her foot, in order to take off her shoe.

"As the SS men stood fascinated, she slammed the high heel of her shoe against the forehead of one of them. While he recoiled in pain, she grabbed his pistol and shot the other German, SS Sergeant Joseph Schillinger, who was noted for his habit of choking inmates to death while they ate their meager meals. He slumped to the floor mortally wounded. In the confusion, the woman wounded another SS man in the leg. Other women clawed at

Hungarian Jews, yellow Stars of David sewn to their clothing, arrive at Auschwitz. At first, Hungary adamantly rejected German requests for the deportation of its Jews. Hitler himself twice protested to the Hungarian government about its "irresolute and ineffective" handling of the Jewish questions. Within a few weeks of the German occupation of Hungary, however, tens of thousands of Hungarian Jews were driven from their towns and villages and forced into ghettos and special camps as a prelude to being transported to the death camps.

the Germans with their bare hands. The changing room was plunged into darkness, and the Germans fled."

Commandant Höss soon arrived. An SS detachment with spotlights, machine guns and grenades surrounded the complex. The Jews in the gas chamber were all executed. Among them was the brave woman, identified only as a dancer from Warsaw named Horowitz. This was the only recorded instance in which someone turned the tables on the Nazi executioners in the shadow of the gas chamber.

Some of the arrivals at Auschwitz were granted a stay of execution. SS physicians made a selection of the incoming deportees at the railroad siding. A doctor would look over the arrivals and classify about one in four as fit for work, most of them men. A jerk of the thumb was the difference between life and death. To the left meant the gas chamber; to the right meant a tattooed identification number on the left forearm, a shaven skull, striped uniform and heavy labor.

In addition to keeping the camp and the crematoriums in operation, work Jews were needed for such profit-making enterprises as its cement factory, gravel works and a wood-products plant. The most labor intensive were the private German industries that sprang up at Auschwitz and its satellite camps. They employed tens of thousands of Jewish inmates and lesser numbers of Polish, Soviet, French and British prisoners of war. Krupp produced detonator fuses for artillery shells, and Siemens, the electrical manufacturer, turned out parts for aircraft and submarines at Auschwitz.

The largest industry at the camp by far was the I.G. Farben complex. The plant, constructed by Jewish slave labor, produced fuel and the ersatz rubber known as Buna from the coal that other inmates mined in the outlying camps. Situated at Monowitz, a few miles east of Auschwitz, the prisoners' compound for plant workers grew so large that it was designated as Auschwitz III. The old main camp became Auschwitz I and Birkenau, farther to the west, was Auschwitz II.

I.G. Farben and the other private companies at Auschwitz paid the SS the equivalent of $1.50 per worker per day, and the camp devoted less than a dime of that to keeping the worker alive. The workers had little nourishment and endured the most primitive sanitary facilities. There were almost no medicines, despite epidemics of typhus and other diseases that ravaged the camp. Prisoners marched to work early in the morning to music from one of the inmate bands. They returned at night carrying their comrades who had collapsed from hunger, overwork or beatings by the overseers, many of whom the SS had recruited from the ranks of German professional criminals.

Inmate labor, to the Germans, was merely an intermediate step on the way to death. Periodically, workers were forced to parade naked before an SS doctor whose thumb sent to the gas chambers anyone he deemed no long fit for labor. The first to go were the *Mussulmans*, prisoners reduced to a zombie-like state by physical and spiritual exhaustion. Jews in good health when they began the work regime typically survived for only about three months.

The SS physicians also chose prisoners to serve as human guinea pigs for medical experiments. Dr. Edmund König studied the effects of electric shock on the brains of teenagers. Dr. Heinz Thilo performed appendectomies and other surgical procedures on healthy subjects to perfect his technique. Research papers detailing experiments, which inflicted pain, maiming or death on thousands, were presented at professional medical meetings in Germany.

An exception was Dr. Wilhelm Hans Münch, a bacteriologist, who tried to help his prisoners. He obtained medicines and supplies and secretly treated sick inmates at the risk of his own life. "One could react like a normal human being in Auschwitz only for the first two hours," he said later. "Once one had spent some time there, it was impossible to react normally. In that atmosphere, everyone was sullied."

Heinrich Himmler was interested in one aspect of the medical research being conducted at Auschwitz—mass sterilization. He dispatched Dr. Carl Clauberg, a leading German gynecologist, to direct a research program at the camp in 1942. He injected various chemicals into the ovaries of Jewish women. Other doctors explored alternative methods. Dr. Horst Schumann subjected both women and men to massive doses of radiation. Dr. Edward Wirths experimented with surgical techniques. All of this produced no medical breakthroughs. Dr. Dora Klein, a prisoner and physician who was forced to serve as a nurse, later said: "I had the feeling that I was in a place that was half hell and half lunatic asylum."

The most memorable physician at Auschwitz was Dr. Joseph Mengele. He was thirty-two when he arrived at the camp in the spring of 1943, after recuperating from wounds suffered on the eastern front. A lover of music and the Italian poet Dante, he exuded a disarming charm, and always wore a fresh uniform—"smelling of a fine soap or eau de cologne," according to a woman survivor.

While many SS physicians so dreaded selections of prisoners that they drank heavily beforehand, Mengele enjoyed the process. He delighted in demonstrating his life-or-death power, and would whistle operatic arias from Wagner as he signaled people to the gas chambers. Once he took aside a group of a hundred rabbis from an arriving train, ordered them to form a large circle and dance for his amusement. Then he waved them to the gas chamber.

Dr. Josef Mengele, whose heinous experiments on inmates at Auschwitz earned him the sobriquet of "the Angel of Death," is shown in Nazi uniform in a rare photograph. The sadistic doctor cut such a dashing figure that some female inmates actually admired him. One prisoner called him a "beautiful person" while others described him as "gorgeous" and even "kindly." He spared twins from the gas chamber for his genetic "studies," and once had twin boys killed so that he could perform autopsies and settle an argument with another doctor. He slipped away just before Auschwitz was liberated and escaped to South America, where he became a figure of notorious legend.

His most bizarre selection came on Yom Kippur, the Jewish Day of Atonement, in 1943. He roared up on his motorcycle at a soccer field where some 2,000 boys had been assembled. He ordered a guard to nail a plank on one of the goalposts and ordered the boys to walk under it. The boys instinctively knew what he was doing: Anyone who did not measure to the marker would be selected for death. "It was 100 percent clear to everyone what the purpose of the game was," recalled Joseph Kleinman, a survivor who had been one of the boys. "We all began stretching. Everyone wanted to get another half-inch, another centimeter."

The young Kleinman stuffed stones and rags in his shoes to add height. When he realized he was still too short, he hid among some taller boys and managed to escape the test. Half the boys failed the test, and were taken away to be gassed. Kleinman later noted that Mengele was literally playing God. He knew of the Jewish prayer, traditionally recited on Yom Kippur, that tells of the flock being led beneath the rod of the shepherd—the Lord—who decides which of them will live.

Mengele volunteered for Auschwitz to pursue research in the biology of racial difference, which happened to be one of Himmler's favorite topics. At Auschwitz, he selected for study about 1,500 sets of identical and fraternal twins, most of them Jewish children, who would receive extra food and a temporary reprieve from the gas chambers for participating in his research.

Using one twin for the control, Mengele would experiment with the other. He took blood, injected chemicals, exposed the subject to radiation, performed experimental surgery, and often ordered one or both twins killed so that he could study them at autopsy.

Vera Kriegel, one of the experimental twins, later described her shock when she saw, at the age of five, the specimens displayed on Mengele's laboratory wall—scores of human eyes "pinned like butterflies." Vera and her sister Olga were among the fewer than 200 twins who survived. Mengele also spared their mother, Vera said, because he "wanted to know why our eyes were brown while our mother's were blue."

Mengele, in attempting to demonstrate the purported genetic degeneracy of Jews, selected people with physical deformities, ordered them executed, and then had their flesh boiled away so that their skeletons could be studied. He discovered a Gypsy family which included seven dwarfs, whom he subjected to painful experiments, then forced them to perform nude before an audience of SS men. The dwarfs became part of what one prisoner described as Mengele's "private zoo."

Two special sections were set up at Auschwitz. One was the Gypsy camp, which housed 10,000 in thirty barracks of Block B2 at Birkenau. It had been established in February, 1942, when Gypsies were first being deported from Germany and Western Europe. The Gypsies lived together as families, and few were put to work outside their compound. For either propaganda purposes, or because of the medical experiments, the Gypsies were spared. But in 1944, Berlin changed its Gypsy policy. Thousands of able-bodied Gypsy prisoners were sent to other camps as slave laborers. The 3,000 remaining were sent to the gas chambers.

Another special section in Birkenau was the family camp in Block B2, originally consisting of some 5,000 Czech Jews. Like the Gypsies, these inmates remained together as families, were spared forced labor and even had their own orchestra. They first arrived in September 1943, from Thereisienstadt, near Prague, a camp that the Nazis referred to as a model ghetto. In truth, it was nothing more than a dressed-up transit and concentration camp. Established in 1942 by emptying the old fortress town of Thereisienstadt of its

*A sign on the high-voltage electric fence at Auschwitz reads: CAUTION. DANGER. Inmates here had more to fear than the fence. Auschwitz was the largest and most notorious of the Vernichtungslager, or extermination camps. Located 150 miles from Warsaw, it was first built in May 1940 as a concentration camp for Polish prisoners. The camp was expanded with an area called Birkenau after the birch trees that stood there. This would become the killing camp. Victims arrived here expecting to be forced to work, or imprisoned, but not killed.*

inhabitants, it was filled with more than 50,000 Jews. They included prominent artists and leaders, veterans of World War I, and the elderly. Most were from the Czech provinces of Bohemia and Moravia. Himmler wanted to create a kind of showcase ghetto to counter stories about the evils of his concentration camps. A propaganda film was made in an attempt to show that the Jews were content and well treated. In truth, some 30,000 people died there of starvation, exposure and disease, and more than twice that number were transported eastward to the death camps.

Most were gassed immediately on arrival at Auschwitz, but a few were diverted to the family camp to continue Himmler's deception. Occupants were allowed to receive parcels from home and encouraged to write postcards to friends and relatives. Representatives of the International Red Cross were allowed to visit the family camp. Typically, after six months in the family camp, a family would be taken to the killing facilities in nearby Birkenau.

The program of deception was so successful that Birkenau was one of the best-kept secrets of the war. It went undetected until mid-1944, despite the word of the mass killings leaking out on several occasions.

One leak came from Lieutenant Kurt Gerstein, the SS officer in Berlin responsible for procuring Zyklon B. He had visited the Reinhard death camps in the summer of 1942, and was shattered by what he saw. On the train home, Gerstein met Baron von Otter, a Swedish diplomat. Gerstein was sweating profusely, and the Swede offered him a cigarette to calm his nerves. "May I tell you a grim story?" Gerstein asked the diplomat.

The SS lieutenant proceeded to tell the diplomat what he had witnessed at Belzec, Sobibor and Treblinka, and presumably the purpose of the poisonous gas he was supplying to Auschwitz. Von Otter sent to Stockholm a detailed report of his startling conversation with Gerstein. The Swedish government, eager to avoid problems with Germany, did not disclose the information.

Britain and the United States soon learned of the death camps. In late 1942, Jan Quarks, a Polish underground courier who had gained firsthand knowledge of the camps, arrived in London with a detailed report. However, the Allies were in no military position to do any more than issue warnings against the "bestial crimes."

Even after the three Reinhard camps had ceased operations, Auschwitz remained shrouded in secrecy. It was the "unknown destination" referred to in many reports of deportations from Western Europe. Isolated references to it made no impression in London and Washington. In fact, on April 4, 1944, an American reconnaissance plane actually flew over Auschwitz and photographed the I.G. Farben synthetic rubber factory at Monowitz. The Buna plant in the Auschwitz main camp showed up clearly, but the killing centers at Birkenau were not recognized for what they were.

By the time the aerial photograph was taken, more than a half-million Jews had been gassed at Auschwitz, and the worst was yet to come. The camp began to prepare for receiving transports from Hungary, the last German-occupied country to deport its Jews. Slave-labor gangs worked around the clock to get ready for that country's estimated 750,000 Jews, whom the SS men referred to as "Hungarian salami." The laborers painted the gas chambers, overhauled the crematoriums, dug five extra cremation pits, and refurbished one of the two old Birkenau farmhouses originally used for gassing. A new three-track rail spur was built to take trains directly to the Birkenau killing complexes.

SS Sergeant Major Otto Möll, who had supervised the burning of the exhumed corpses in 1942, was appointed overseer of all the crematoriums. Möll, a short, thickset man with freckles and a glass eye, wore a white uniform and liked to boast that he would burn his own wife and seven-year-old child if so ordered by the Führer. He was fond of such practices as hurling live babies into the burning pits and using naked young women for target practice.

Commandant Höss knew Möll to be a ruthlessly efficient organizer, the sort he needed to speed the disposal of the expected deluge of Hungarian Jews. Moll was already making improvements. In the new cremation pits he had laborers digging out drainage channels that were sloped so that the fat from the burning bodies would run down and collect in pans. The fat could then be poured back onto the fire and make it burn faster.

# Chapter 13

*We wanted once to see a killed German.*
*Then we could sleep better.*
*That is why we enjoyed the bombing.*

**Arie Hassenberg**
**an Auschwitz work Jew**

Hungary joined the Axis early in the war in the hope of annexing neighboring territory, but Hitler became dissatisfied with the country's performance, particularly in its handling of the Jewish question. The chief of state, Admiral Míklos Horthy, repeatedly refused to deport the country's Jews, which comprised the largest Jewish community surviving in occupied Europe.

By 1944, Horthy was hoping to make a separate peace with the Allies, and didn't want to jeopardize his position by deporting the Jews. Hitler reacted by sending troops into Hungary on March 19. A few days later, Adolf Eichmann arrived to supervise the deportation. He told Jewish leaders to establish a Jewish council to carry out his orders. Then he began concentrating the Jews into makeshift ghettos.

On May 15, deportations began. Despite the advancing Red Army, trains serving the Eastern front were diverted to Hungary. The transports typically consisted of more than forty sealed freight cars. As many as a hundred Jews were crammed into each car with one bucket of drinking water and one waste bucket for a journey of 200 miles, which sometimes took four days. At Auschwitz, the trains rolled onto the new spur right up to the Birkenau crematoriums.

Only a few of the early Hungarian deportees were selected for the labor gangs. The writer Elie Wiesel, then fourteen years old, was one of the lucky few, selected along with his father to work at the I. G. Farben rubber factory. But he later wrote that as they stood in line after the selection, no one knew for sure which of the two lines led to work and which to death.

"Around us," Wiesel wrote, "everyone was weeping. Someone began to recite the *Kaddish*, the Hebrew prayer for the dead. I do not know if it has ever happened before, in the long history of the Jews, that people have ever recited the prayer for the dead for themselves."

As the early arrivals at Auschwitz entered the disrobing rooms, they were handed postcards. SS men ordered them to write home that they had arrived at "Waldsee," a mythical camp where they had found work and lacked for nothing. These postcards had the desired effect when they arrived in Hungary. Moshe Sandberg, whose family received such a card from his father, later wrote: "The postcards acted as a sleeping drug, coming just at the right time to tranquilize us, to dispel the accumulated misgivings of the past few weeks, and to remove any thought of revolt or escape."

The killing complexes operated as never before. Within two months, from May to July 1944, almost 440,000 Hungarian Jews were deported and most of them were immediately put to death at Birkenau. To dispose of their remains, the crematorium crews of the *Sonderkommando* were quadrupled and employed 900 work Jews. Smoke from the chimneys and the open burning pits blotted out the sun.

As the killings reached a peak, the Allies at last became aware of what was happening at Auschwitz. Eyewitness accounts from escaped prisoners reached London and Washington. The reports of Rudolf Vrba and Alfred Wetzler, both Slovaks, told in detail the gassing procedures at Birkenau. Statements by Arnost Rosin, a Slovak, and Czeslaw Mordowicz, a Pole, described the arrival and the killing of the Hungarian Jews. Prime Minister Winston Churchill was moved to write an associate, "There is no doubt that this is probably the greatest and most horrible crime ever committed in the whole history of the world."

Hungary's Admiral Horthy was caught in a storm of protests. Messages urging him to stop the deportations came from the President of the International Red Cross, the King of Sweden and the Pope. More disturbing to Horthy were intercepted British and American messages raising the possibility of bombing raids on government offices in Budapest and possible reprisals against prominent Hungarian officials. On July 9 Horthy ordered the deportations halted.

Jewish leaders throughout the free world urged the British and Americans to initiate a bombing campaign to destroy the Birkenau killing centers and disrupt the rail traffic between Hungary and Auschwitz. The Allies refused. If gas chambers were bombed, military leaders explained, the Germans would find other means of carrying out the Final Solution. Targeting Birkenau would only divert Allied air forces from their mission of destroying the strategic industries that sustained the Nazi war machine.

On August 20, American B-17 bombers actually hit Auschwitz, making the first of four attacks on the I. G. Farben facility at Monowitz, a few miles east of the gas chambers. The bombing stirred hope and joy among the 30,000 Jewish slave laborers at the plant even though they were doubly endangered. "We wanted once to see a killed German," recalled, Arie Hassenberg, one of the survivors. "Then we could sleep better. That was why we enjoyed the bombing."

Hassenberg got his wish less than a month later. Bombs from American B-24's attacking I.G. Farben on September 13, fell short and destroyed a barracks at the main camp at Auschwitz. Fifteen SS men were killed and twenty-eight wounded. A cluster of bombs also fell by mistake on Birkenau, damaging the railroad but missing the crematoria.

An unusual rescue mission was being mounted in Budapest during the summer and fall of 1944. The participants included diplomats from five neutral nations—Portugal, Spain, Sweden, Turkey and Switzerland—along with the Papal Nuncio and representatives of the International Red Cross. In an attempt to save the nearly 200,000 Jews remaining in Budapest from the resumption of deportations to Auschwitz, they issued thousands of diplomatic letters of protection intended to safeguard the bearers, and then secured the Jews who received them in hundreds of specially designated apartment buildings.

Working with the Jewish underground in Budapest, three foreigners led this unprecedented mission of mercy. One was Charles Lutz, the Swiss counsel, a forty-nine-year-old career diplomat who was instrumental in issuing more than 8,000 safe-conduct passes, and assisted the underground in setting up an operation to print tens of thousands of additional passes.

Another was Giorgio Perlasca, an Italian meat importer who himself had sought protection from the Spanish embassy in Budapest after the overthrow of Mussolini made Italians suspect in Axis countries. Bearing a diplomatic passport, Perlasca helped the Spanish Embassy issue letters of protection and set up safe houses for some 5,200 Jews. He continued his work even after the approach of the Red Army forced the closing of the Spanish Embassy. Perlasca solved the problem by appointing himself the Spanish Chargé d'affaires.

A key figure in the rescue effort was Raoul Wallenberg. The thirty-two-year-old Swede, a member of a family of prominent bankers, industrialists and diplomats, was a charming and cultured executive in an import-export firm. His ancestral connections to Judaism were slight: a great-great-grandfather had been a German Jew. Wallenberg was the attaché of the Swedish legation, but his primary task was to help the Jews on behalf of the War Refugee Board, a new agency of the U.S. government.

Arriving in Budapest the day the deportations were halted, Wallenberg began to issue the Swedish safe-conduct passes. Like the passes handed out by

*Swedish diplomat Raoul Wallenberg, shown at work at his desk, is credited with saving 20,000 Hungarian Jews by his bold and courageous work. An aristocrat and the scion of a distinguished banking family, he knew Jews from serving the Haifa branch of the family bank. Under the auspices of the Red Cross, he went to Budapest in 1944 as Jews were being sent to the death camps. He plucked Jews out of death marches, removed them from ghettos, issued them counterfeit passports, and helped protect 70,000 confined Jews who survived until liberation.*

the Swiss, Spanish and other legations, his passes had no real standing or precedent under international law. But Wallenberg proved so adept at cajoling and bribing Hungarian officials that the government formally recognized and respected the passes.

In mid-October, the Germans engineered the overthrow of Admiral Horthy after he attempted to negotiate a separate peace with the Soviet Union, whose forces already had entered Hungary. The SS installed the Hungarian fascist extremists known as the Arrow Cross and brought back Adolf Eichmann to resume deportations.

Wallenberg, now aided by a staff of nearly 400 Hungarian Jews, negotiated for the creation of an "international ghetto" where thousands of Jews were housed under the protection of the neutral legations. He would race to the rail yards to rescue Jews with Swedish passports from Auschwitz-bound trains, even climbing on the roof of the cars to distribute passes to those who lacked them.

When Eichmann, faced with a shortage of rail cars, began marching thousands of Jews to slave labor camps in Austria, Wallenberg and the Swiss diplomat Charles Lutz, drove along the route of march, boldly pulling from the ranks hundreds of Jews who carried protective papers.

In Budapest, some 100,000 Jews were in safe houses maintained by the neutral legations. They remained safe from deportation until the Soviet liberation of Budapest in January, 1945. Shortly after the liberation, however, Raoul Wallenberg was arrested by the Russians on suspicion of espionage and simply vanished. Even though a decade after the war the Russians reported that Wallenberg had died in a Soviet prison in 1947, his definitive fate remains unknown.

A rescue operation of a different sort met with success in Poland. Oskar Schindler, a native of the Sudetenland, went to Krakow in late 1939 in the wake of the German invasion, and took over two Jewish firms that manufactured kitchenware. He then established his own company outside Krakow, where he employed mostly Jewish workers, which protected them from deportation.

When the Krakow ghetto was liquidated in early 1943, many Jews were sent to the Plaszow labor camp, which was infamous for the brutality of its commandant, Amon Goeth. Schindler used his connections with high German officials to open a small armament plant in the camp which employed some 900 Jews, including many who were unfit for other assignments in the camp.

In October, 1944, as the Red Army approached, Schindler was allowed to reestablish his armament plant at Brunnlitz in the Sudetenland and take his Jewish workers with him. In an operation unequaled in occupied Europe, he effectively freed 800 Jewish men from the Gross Rosen camp and 300 Jewish women from Auschwitz. In Brunnlitz, the Jews were given the most humane treatment possible—adequate food, medical care and religious needs.

Schindler learned that a train with evacuated Jewish prisoners from the Goleszow camp were stranded at the nearby Svitavy railroad station. He went there, had the sealed train doors forced open and removed a hundred nearly frozen Jewish men and women, and took them to his Brunnlitz facility, where he was able to nurse most of them back to life.

Throughout the war, Schindler had maintained friends in the German military and in high government positions, and managed to ingratiate himself with high-ranking SS commanders in Poland. He used all these connections

to extract crucial favors from them, such as easing conditions for prisoners under his care. He was himself imprisoned on several occasions, only to be released through the intervention of his important friends.

Meanwhile, at Auschwitz, Jews stopped arriving from Hungary and the *Sonderkommando* at the killing complexes were thrown into turmoil. The crews knew that they were living on borrowed time. When the trains ceased to arrive, their usefulness—and their lives—would come to an end. "It stood to reason," wrote Filip Müller, "that the perpetrators of daily mass murders would not allow a single witness of their crimes to stay alive and to testify against them."

Müller and the others realized that they must escape or die. During the spring and summer of 1944, while nearly 400,000 Hungarian Jews were being gassed, the *Sonderkommando* developed elaborate plans for an uprising and mass escape. They obtained small arms from workers in the camp shops where downed airplanes were dismantled. They arranged with female Jewish workers at the munitions factory to smuggle out explosives in the false bottoms of food trays.

Plans for an uprising were coordinated with the campwide underground movement whose leadership was dominated by Polish gentiles. However, the camp resistance leaders repeatedly postponed the uprising. The Red Army was advancing from the east, and they were inclined to sit tight until they were liberated.

By early fall 1944, the anxiety level of the crematoria crews reached the breaking point. With the transports from Hungary still halted, Sergeant Major Möll and the SS overseers decided to reduce the 863-man *Sonderkommando*. During the last week in September, they chose 200 members and gassed them. A week or so later, the names of 300 additional workers were placed on a new selection list, supposedly for transfer to another camp. Despite the objections of the camp underground and their comrades in the crematoria, those on the list decided to strike immediately.

The revolt erupted about noon, October 7, in the yard outside Crematorium IV. The SS men were conducting a roll call to cull the prisoners on the selection list when they were pelted with a flurry of stones thrown by the prisoners who had been selected. Other workers hidden inside the crematorium set fire to rags soaked in oil and wood alcohol, and soon the building was ablaze. Truckloads of SS guards roared up to surround the yard and began firing. But the wail of the camp siren and the leaping flames alerted the work crews in two other crematoriums. They seized the weapons and explosives they had stashed away and raced to cut through the inner cordon of barbed wire around Birkenau.

Few of the inmates got far. Some 450 of them died during the uprising— half again as many as were scheduled to be gassed that day. Later, the SS men hanged the four female workers who had helped furnish the explosives. But three SS men had been killed and one crematorium destroyed. The inmates had staged what Filip Müller later described as "a unique event in the history of Auschwitz."

The killings went on. The trains from Hungary stopped coming, but victims arrived from other parts of Europe. Throughout October, Jews died at the rate of more than a thousand a day. On October 30, the last trainload of Jews arrived from Theresienstadt, and 1,689 of them were processed at the killing center.

Then, on November 2, 1944, more than three years after the first gassing experiments at Auschwitz, an order arrived at the death camp from Heinrich Himmler: "I forbid any further annihilation of Jews." Upon further orders, all but one of the crematoria were dismantled, the burning pits covered up and planted with grass, and the gas pipes and other equipment shipped to concentration camps in Germany. The single remaining crematorium was for the disposal of those who died natural deaths and the gassing of about 200 surviving members of the *Sonderkommando*.

The Final Solution was almost over. While thousands of Jews and others would still die of neglect and brutality, the systematic killing had ended. Why did Himmler make this decision? Evidence suggests that Himmler foresaw the disaster that awaited the Third Reich and was desperately trying to save his own skin by compiling a record of what possibly could be termed "leniency." Ironically, his order to stop the killing also instructed that "proper care be given to the weak and the sick."

*Theresiendtadt.*

On January 17, 1945, less than three months after Himmler's directive, the last roll call was conducted at Auschwitz. The remaining prisoners, nearly 60,000, were forcibly marched back to Greater Germany; most died on these death marches. Many had to march all the way to Germany in freezing cold. Staggering along in rags, barefoot or in wooden clogs, sustained only by a starvation diet, thousands fell by the wayside and were shot by their SS guards. One march lasted for more than sixteen weeks and claimed the lives of all but 280 of the 3,000 who began it. Even those put aboard trains underwent privation. Many hundreds died of starvation or exposure in the unheated cars.

At Auschwitz, those left behind were without food, water or heat, and they died by the hundreds each day. The SS guards slowly disappeared by increments, until finally the inmates had the camp to themselves. The Russians arrived on January 27, "a beautiful, sunny winter's day," according to a survivor. "At about 3:00 p.m., we heard a noise in the direction of the main gate. We hurried to the scene. It was a Soviet forward patrol—Soviet soldiers in white caps! There was a mad rush to shake them by the hand and shout our gratitude. We were liberated!"

By then, only about 2,800 people remained alive at Auschwitz. The Soviet soldiers fed the survivors, tended to the sick and buried the dead. One inmate observed that this mass burial was the "first dignified funeral" ever held there. For reasons unknown, the Soviets downplayed the liberation of Auschwitz. The story was not reported until May, after Soviet troops had liberated Majdanek, Sachsenhausen, Ravensbrück, Stütthof and Theresienstadt.

The soldiers found the evidence of genocide at Auschwitz. In storehouses the SS had failed to torch were hundreds of thousands of women's coats and dresses, men's suits, and seven tons of human hair. As dozens of other Nazi concentration camps were liberated by the advancing Allied armies, more and more evidence was unearthed: emaciated corpses, ashes, bits of bone, clothing. In the end, Heinrich Himmler had been unable to keep the secret of the Final Solution. Soon the world would have to confront the reality of the Holocaust.

# Chapter 14

*I only took part in this crime because there was nothing I could do to change anything.*

## Maximillian Grabner
### head of the Political Department at Auschwitz testifying at his trial in Krakow.

When British troops entered Bergen-Belsen on April 15, 1945, the camp commandant, Joseph Kramer, greeted them in a fresh uniform. He expressed his desire for an orderly transition and his hopes of collaborating with the British. Kramer treated the British officers as equals, even offering them advice on dealing with the "unpleasant" situation. Touring the camp, Derrick Singleton, a junior officer remarked, "You've made a fine hell here." The commandant replied, "It has become one in the last few days."

An epidemic of typhus raged through the camp. Thousands of bodies lay rotting in the sun. About 60,000 inmates were still alive, but many of them were in critical condition. In the first days of freedom, 14,000 died and as many again died in the weeks that followed. Even for prisoners who arrived from Birkenau, conditions in Bergen-Belsen were severe. The epidemic was so lethal that the camp had to be burned down. The survivors were moved to a Panzer training school two miles down the road, which became the site of a displaced-persons camp.

Mass graves were dug and bulldozers pushed the bodies into them. Local civilians were marched into the camp and taken on a tour. Before they began their visit, a British colonel told them: ". . . What you will see here is the final and utter condemnation of the Nazi Party. It justifies every measure the United Nations will take to exterminate that party. What you will see here is such a disgrace to the German people that their names must be erased from the list of civilized nations . . . ." Films of Bergen-Belsen taken by the British were shown throughout the world and made the name Bergen-Belsen unforgettable. In September 1945, forty-eight members of the camp staff were put on trial for war crimes. Eleven, including Commandant Kramer, were executed the following December.

American troops entered Buchenwald on April 11, 1945, a few days after 25,000 prisoners were taken out of the camp. Many of them did not survive. Other camps liberated by Americans that month included Nordhausen, Ohrdruf, Landsberg, Woebblein, Gunskirchen, Ebensee and Flossenburg. As American troops approached Dachau on April 29, an inmate, Piet Maas, wrote in his diary: "17:28 [5:28 p.m.]. First American comes through the entrance. Dachau free!!! Indescribable happiness. Insane howling."

The last camp liberated by the Americans was Mauthausen on May 5, 1945. Three days later Germany surrendered. Now a new battle began—a battle to bring the Holocaust survivors back to life. One survivor of Bergen-Belsen wrote: "For the great part of the liberated Jews of Bergen-Belsen, there was no ecstasy, no joy at our liberation. We had lost our families, our homes. We had no place to go, nobody to hug, nobody who was waiting for us, anywhere. We had been liberated from death and from the fear of death, but we were not free from the fear of life."

As the Allied armies closed in on Berlin, Hitler retreated to the Reich Chancellory's two-story air-raid shelter fifty feet below ground. On April 22, Soviet troops entered the devastated city. Hitler's entourage was nervous and exhausted. Some were near hysteria. Hitler was unable to sleep. Some of his staff, including Hermann Göring, had fled south. Himmler had begun discussions with Count Bernadotte of Sweden, who told him the Allies were insisting on unconditional surrender. Word of Himmler's attempted negotiations were leaked to Hitler.

In his final hours, Hitler married Eva Braun, his longtime companion. After the ceremony and a brief celebration, he dictated his final testament. He expelled Himmler and Göring from the Nazi party, named Admiral Dönitz President of the Reich, Goebbels as Chancellor, and Bormann as Party Minister. His final lines were addressed to the unfinished Final Solution: "Above all I charge the leaders of the nation and those under them to scrupulous observance of the laws of race and to merciless opposition to the universal poisoner of all peoples, international Jewry."

Within twenty-four hours, Eva Braun had taken poison, and Hitler had shot himself in the mouth. Their bodies were burned outside the bunker. The Führer and his thousand-year Reich had come to an end.

In the winter of 1943, Churchill, Roosevelt and Stalin had announced that as soon as the war was over they would bring the Nazi leaders to justice. Within weeks after the Red Army liberated the first death camps, the first trials of Nazi war criminals were begun by the Soviets at Majdanek.

Two weeks after the German surrender, an agreement was reached by the Allies to conduct joint trials of those responsible for the murder of millions of

*Although he often appeared to be little more than a wily bureaucrat, Martin Bormann, a confidant to Hitler and his deputy for party affairs, wielded great power. Bormann served as secretary at secret meetings where Hitler harangued about the persecution of the Jews and the slave labor camps. A German intelligence officer would describe Bormann as "the evil genius behind the Führer's commands." Ironically, his detailed records would form the damning record that would convict Nazis at the Nuremberg trials. He was reported killed attempting to escape Berlin during the last days of the war, although reports persisted that he was alive in South America.*

noncombatants. Justice Robert Jackson of the United States Supreme Court was selected to lead the American prosecution. Nuremberg, the site chosen for the trials, was one of the few German cities not totally in ruins. It also had been the host to the annual Nazi party pageants.

Three kinds of crimes were specified in the indictments. First were Crimes Against the Peace, which included planning, preparing, initiating or waging a war of aggression. Second were War Crimes, acts that violated the laws and customs of warfare. This category covered the murder, ill-treatment or deportation of populations for slave labor or any other purposes; the killing of hostages and prisoners of war; the plunder of private property; and the destruction of towns and cities.

Finally there were Crimes Against Humanity. These were defined as the murder, extermination, enslavement or deportations of any civilian popu-

*This is what starvation looks like. The Hungarian Jew in the foreground had been starved to near death before his camp was liberated. In most camps, healthy male prisoners were put into labor battalions, worked from dawn to dusk, and fed a diet below subsistence level. Little matter if the prisoners died within months; more were constantly arriving. Starvation and disease, particularly typhus, killed more prisoners in the camps than did the gas chambers.*

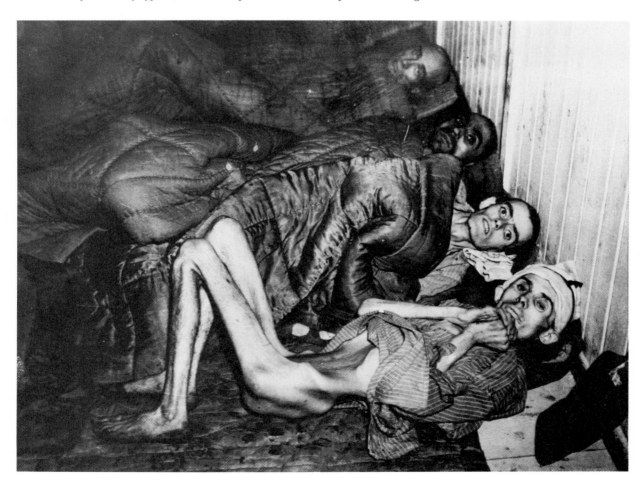

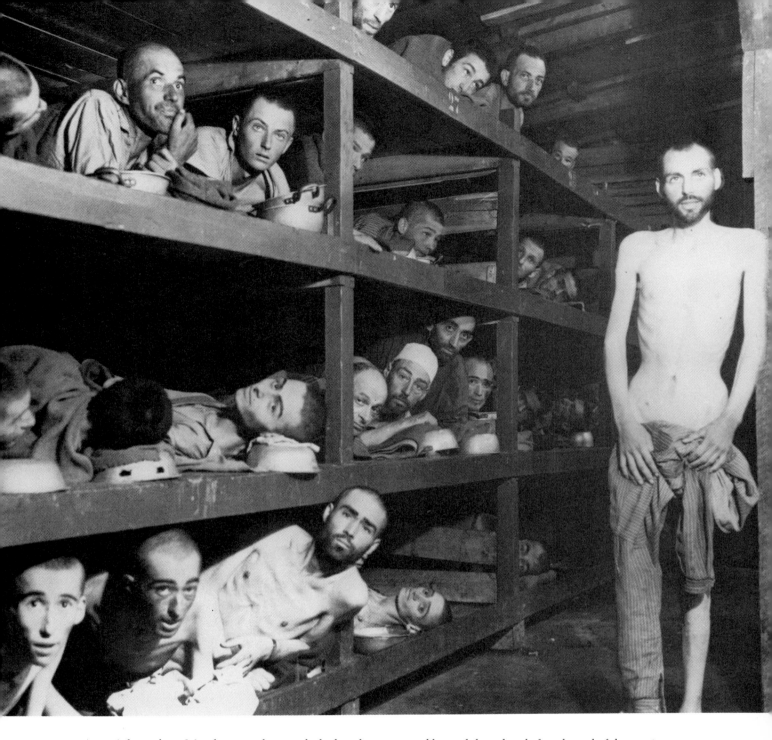

A men's barracks at Mauthausen, photographed when the camp was liberated three days before the end of the war in Europe. In January 1945, hours before the Red Army arrived at Auschwitz, 66,000 prisoners were marched to Wodzislaw, Poland, and brought by train to this and other camps. Almost one in four died en route. There were many death marches. In 1941, hundreds of thousands of Soviet prisoners of war were herded along the highways of the Ukraine and Belorussia from one camp to another. In 1942 Jews were marched from small ghettos to larger ghettos, only to be sent from there to the death camps. There were fifty-nine marches from camps during the final winter of the war, some covering hundreds of miles. The prisoners were given little or no food or water, and hardly any time to rest. Those who paused or fell behind were shot. Many simply reached the end of their strength and collapsed.

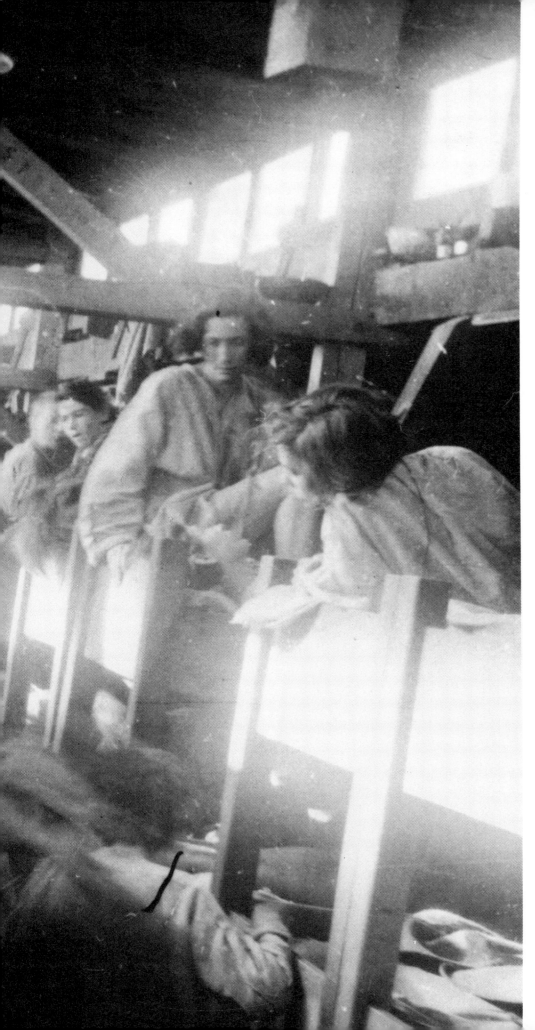

A women's barracks at Mauthausen, photographed on the day of liberation—the inmates still trying to accept that their ordeal had ended. When American troops reached Mauthausen, they found nearly 10,000 bodies in a huge communal grave. Of the 110,000 survivors, more than 3,000 died after liberation. Some died because they were too weak or sick to be nursed back to health, others because they left the camp before they were strong enough to begin normal life again. The Austrian camp was notorious for its stone quarry, the center of its forced labor network.

*This photograph of Dachau, made after the camp was liberated, gives no hint of what awaited the first American troops who arrived on April 29, 1945. The soldiers were infuriated by the piles of decomposing bodies lying around the camp. The stink of death was everywhere. One soldier recalled: "Control was gone after the sights we saw, and the men were deliberately wounding guards that were available and then turning them over to prisoners and allowing them to take their revenge on them." SS officers were paraded through the barracks. Prisoners were asked to judge. The questions were simple: good or bad? The judgment was carried out immediately.*

lation; persecution on political, racial or religious grounds, whether or not these were in violation of the domestic laws of the country where the acts took place.

Trials which took place in 1946 were deemed International Military Tribunals. Twenty-two major Nazi leaders were indicted and placed on trial by the Allies, including Hitler's trusted lieutenant Hermann Göring; Nazi party officials; the foreign minister and other key cabinet officials; military leaders; the ministers of armaments and labor; ranking bureaucrats; and German occupation officials, including Hans Frank, the governor-general of Poland and Fritz Sauckel, who had run the slave-labor program.

Some key figures were missing from the courtroom dramas. Goebbels and his wife had committed suicide after killing their children. Himmler killed

*Soldiers see the calcinated corpses at the Ohrdruf concentration camp, the first to be liberated by American forces. This was a Nazi slave-labor camp near the underground V-2 rocket factories, thirty-seven miles southwest of Buchenwald. Toughened by combat, the soldiers had seen all the horrors of war—ferocious infantry fighting, the destruction of bombing raids, the ugliness of death. But on entering the camps they stumbled into a world beyond anything they had seen or could have imagined. One American officer described his first impressions: "As we burst into the camp and spread out, I saw in front of me a row of wooden one-story barracks . . . One of my men came for me. 'You'd better come with me.' His voice was very serious. I followed him across the yard to a building . . . The windows were all sealed up. Outside . . . eight automobiles, all up on blocks . . . The exhausts were piped in through the wall of that building. We went inside the door. In the room . . . there was human excretion, vomit, urine, blood all over the room. I did not understand. And there were shower heads and faucets, all over the wall. One of my men called out to me. He said: 'What the hell's going on here?' He said: 'There's no water.' We entered the back room filled with benches and tables. And on one of the tables there were thousands of gold wedding rings . . . piles of human teeth with gold fillings . . . It was obvious that someone was there counting them. We went outside into the yard. In front of me I could see human hair. There were piles of boots, shoes, suitcases, eyeglasses. To my left were four-wheel hay wagons and two-wheel push carts. These wagons contained nude bodies . . . men, women and children, even babies. All nude, all dead, all piled as high as they basically could pile them."*

*The burned, emaciated bodies of Jewish prisoners lie in the rain outside their smoldering hut at the Landsberg concentration camp, southwest of Nuremberg in Bavaria. The huts were set afire with the prisoners inside by Nazi guards before they fled in advance of the U.S. Seventh Army. Apparently, they had sufficient strength to crawl outside before succumbing to the flames. Burned fragments of clothing still cling to the corpses. As Germany was nearing defeat, there were attempts in the camps to destroy the evidence and make sure no one was left to testify against the administrators and the guards.*

himself after he was captured. Dr. Robert Ley, who headed the Reich Labor Front, hanged himself in his cell.

The opening statement of Justice Jackson set the tone of the tribunal: "In the prisoners' dock sit twenty-odd broken men. Reproached by the humiliation of those they have led almost as bitterly as the desolation of those they have attacked, their personal capacity for evil is forever past. It is hard now to perceive in these miserable men as captives the power by which as Nazi leaders they once dominated much of the world and terrified most of it. Merely as individuals, their fate is of little consequence to the world."

"What makes this inquest significant is that these prisoners . . . are the living symbols of racial hatreds, of terrorism and violence, and of the arrogance and cruelty of power . . . Civilization can afford no compromise with the social forces which would gain renewed strength if we deal ambiguously or indecisively with the men in whom those forces precariously survive."

Of the twenty-one who stood trial, fourteen, including Göring, were sentenced to death by hanging. The remaining seven received prison sentences. (Before he could be hanged, however, Göring committed suicide with poison smuggled into his cell.)

After the Military Tribunals were concluded, a second series of trials took place in Germany. The 185 defendants were divided into twelve groups. Physicians were tried for their complicity in the selection, murder and medical experimentation that took place in the camps. Officers of the mobile killing units were prosecuted for the slaughter of civilians in Eastern Europe. Camp administrators were tried for the systematic murders that occurred under their supervision. Judges were tried for the complicity in the transformation of German law into an instrument of mass murder. The generals who invaded the Soviet Union were placed on trial. Top executives of I. G. Farben were

The day after Buchenwald was liberated by American troops, an inmate, persecuted beyond the limit of his endurance, sits on a pile of filthy blankets, overwhelmed by an uncertain future. Freedom from the camps did not necessarily mean survival. At first, the people in the displaced persons camps were young single men. Few women and fewer old people had survived. The refugee camps were poorly run. An American army major wrote home: "The camp is filthy beyond description. Sanitation is virtually unknown . . . The Army units we relieved obviously did nothing more than insure that rations were delivered to the camp. With few exceptions the people of the camp themselves appear demoralized beyond hope of rehabilitation. They appear to be beaten both spiritually and physically."

tried for the sale of Zyklon B and the construction of industrial plants at Auschwitz. Alfred Krupp and the directors of his company were tried for their use of slave labor. Other industrialists, officers who had held hostages and soldiers, made up the remaining six trials.

The defendants did not deny they had done these things. A few professed ignorance, claiming they did not know what was happening. Others complained that they were being singled out, that many others who were still at large had done exactly the same deeds. The most common defense was to deny responsibility, to insist they had merely been following orders. If anyone was responsible, they declared, it was someone further up the chain of command. Generals and judges invoked the personal oath of allegiance they had sworn to Hitler. As men of morality, they lamented, they were obliged to obey because they had given their word of honor to the Führer.

*Services are held for the victims of Nazi atrocities and some 500 German civilians and a group of American soldiers look on. The German pastor conducting the services said local residents were unaware of the atrocities. It became American army policy to make sure German civilians became aware of the atrocities. They were brought to the camps and made to walk by the piles of unburied corpses, and were sometimes compelled to assist in burying them.*

Defendants who were directly involved in the mass killings—camp commandants, *Einsatzgruppen* officers, camp doctors—received the most severe sentences. Guilty industrialists were treated more leniently. Thirty-five of the other defendants were acquitted.

The trials were held against the background of the unfolding Cold War. The 1948 Berlin Blockade made the future of Germany central to American interests, which made the American government reluctant to provoke the German people, and the Korean War intensified the American desire to get the trials over with quickly.

Almost as soon as the trials ended, clemency boards were established. Over the next few years, sentences were reduced, pardons were granted, and time off was given for good behavior. In 1948, thirty-seven death sentences were commuted, leaving only six war criminals remaining under sentences of death. A general amnesty was issued in 1951 by the U.S. High Commissioner for Germany, John J. McCloy, who, in 1944 as Assistant Secretary of War had pushed for the war-crimes trial. McCloy had been under great pressure. The representative of the Pope and Konrad Adenauer were among those who pressed for amnesty.

Some Nazi leaders had gone underground and taken on new identities. Others had fled to South America or to the Middle East where they took refuge among the enemies of Israel. The Nazi escape route, called the Rat Line, led from Austria and Bavaria over the mountains into Italy and from there to South America. Fleeing Nazis were helped along the way by ODESSA, an organization of SS men formed for this express purpose. Some Nazis were aided by Western intelligence agencies that wanted to employ them in the global battle against Communism.

Rome became a sanctuary for fleeing Nazis. Bishop Alois Hudal, rector of the German Church in Rome, had protested the deportation of Jews and sheltered a number of them. Yet he also assisted a number of Nazi war criminals, including Eichmann, Walther Rauff (chief of the SS in Milan), Otto Wachter (the governor of Galicia who was responsible for the murder of 800,000 Jews) and the infamous Josef Mengele.

Many Nazi war criminals came to the United States, posing as anti-Communists fleeing Soviet persecution in Eastern Europe. The U.S. government also employed Nazis and helped them enter the country. Operation Paperclip, a project run by the Joint Chiefs of Staff, brought German and Austrian scientists and technicians, including many war criminals, to the military and NASA. Arthur Rudolph, the director of the Saturn V moon rocket project, used slave labor at the Dora concentration camp when he was in charge of a V-2 rocket factory.

An American soldier, Cpl. Larry Mutinsk of Philadelphia, distributes cigarettes to prisoners within the stockade at Dachau. An Army journalist descried the liberation of Dachau: "It was late afternoon—about 4 p.m.—as the men made their way down the tracks. They knew that camp ahead was guarded by SS troops and that they expected a hard fight. And like all men going into an attack, be they rookies or vets, these men were afraid. They picked up the clawing stink before they reached the first boxcar. They stopped and stared and the dead stared back. There were about a dozen bodies in the dirty boxcar, men and women alike. They had gone without food so long that their dead wrists were broomsticks tipped with claws . . . The men looked, then shuffled on to the new car in silence. There were more dead eyes here staring out at the German houses not 200 yards from the tracks. Someone broke the stillness with a curse and then with a roar the men started for the camp on the double. 'I never saw anything like it,' an officer said later. "The men were plain fighting mad. They went down that road without any regard for cover or concealment. No one was afraid, not after those boxcars. We were just mad."

*Generals Dwight D. Eisenhower, Omar Bradley and George Patton view the emaciated corpses of concentration camp prisoners on a visit to Ohrdruf. U.S. troops liberated the camp, southwest of Berlin, on April 4, 1945, only to learn that hundreds of prisoners had been shot on the eve of the American arrival. After his visit to the camp, Eisenhower sent photographs of the dead prisoners to Churchill, who at once arranged for several members of Parliament to visit the camp.*

Had the Nuremberg trials accomplished anything? Yes, for the first time in history, a nation's leaders had been held legally accountable for crimes committed in the course of carrying out their government's responsibility. They were not absolved by the defense that they were only carrying out orders.

War criminals were prosecuted in many European countries, and many collaborators were persecuted, including Prime Minister Pierre Laval of the French Vichy government, Presidents Tiso of Slovakia and Bagrianov of Bulgaria, Marshal Antonescu of Romania, and General Sztojay of Hungary.

German civilians are forced to help bury the corpses of inmates found when this unidentified camp was liberated. Practically all Germans denied having any knowledge of what went on in the camps, although the odor of burning flesh was detectable for miles around. Under American occupation policy, Germans were taken through the camps to see for themselves what their leaders had wrought. Even hardened Red Army soldiers were appalled. One Soviet correspondent wrote: "In the course of my travels into liberated territory I have never seen a more abominable sight than Majdanek near Lublin . . . where more than half a million European men, women and children were massacred. . . . This is not a concentration camp, it is a giant murder plant. . . . In the center of the camp stands a huge stone building with a factory chimney—the world's biggest crematorium . . . The gas chambers contained some 250 people at a time. They were closely packed . . . so that after they suffocated they remained standing . . . It is difficult to believe it myself but human eyes cannot deceive me."

*A rabbi from the U.S. Army Chaplain Corps holds Jewish services in Schloss Rheydt Castle in München-Gladback, Germany, which had just been occupied by troops of the 29th Division of the Ninth Army. These were the first Jewish services held east of the Ruhr River since well before the war, and were offered in memory of the Jewish soldiers in the American army who lost their lives in the fighting in Germany. A captured swastika is a grim reminder of the horrors meted out to the European Jews by the Nazis.*

The Soviet Union tried thirteen Soviet citizens who had served in mobile killing units. Similar trials were held in Kharkov in 1943 and in Majdanek immediately following its liberation in 1944.

Poland tried those who presided over the destruction of the ghettos in Warsaw, Lublin and Lodz. Thousands of collaborators were prosecuted, and the Polish Main Commission for the Investigation of Nazi War Crimes was still in operation forty-five years after the war. In Rumania and Hungary, war criminals were tried en masse. The Norwegians tried Vidkun Quisling, their wartime prime minister. In Holland and France, many war criminals were tried in the years immediately following the war. In 1988, Klaus Barbie, who had been responsible for the deportations of Jews from Lyon, was finally brought to trial.

*On the first anniversary of the liberation of Dachau by the Seventh Army, prisoners reenact the happy event by raising a homemade American flag. Originally considered a photograph of the actual liberation, researchers changed their minds after noting that the men appeared well fed and seemed to be bursting out of their camp uniforms. In the last year of the war more than 40,000 prisoners died at Dachau. After the war, the camp was used as a prison for Nazi war criminals. At a series of trials in the town of Dachau, 260 former SS functionaries were sentenced to death and executed.*

In West Germany, prosecutors investigated about 91,000 Germans accused of being Nazi war criminals, convicting 6,479 of them. Twelve were sentenced to death; 160 to life imprisonment. In East Germany, nearly 13,000 war criminals were convicted.

In 1979, the U.S. Department of Justice established an Office of Special Investigations to track down Nazi war criminals who had found refuge in the United States. Similar investigations were conducted in Great Britain, Australia and Canada.

*Justice finally caught up with Adolf Eichmann, the architect of the Final Solution, in a courtroom in Jerusalem in 1961. He sat in a protective glass booth, at left in the photograph, charged with crimes against humanity, crimes against the Jewish people, and crimes in violation of international laws in the conduct of war. As the days wore on, Israeli prosecutors extracted another long chapter in the well-*

documented Nazi war against the Jews. Eichmann pleaded that he was only following orders. "Why me?" he asked at his trial. But the court found that it was Eichmann who had been the bureaucratic murderer of millions of Jews. He was found guilty and sentenced to death. Eichmann was hanged on May 31, 1962.

In 1960, Israel captured Adolf Eichmann in Argentina, and forcibly brought him to Israel for trial. The capture and trial of Eichmann, the SS official in charge of the deportation of the Jews, was controversial. In his capture, Israel had violated the sovereignty of another state. Eichmann was tried before Jewish justices in the tribunal of a state that did not exist when Eichmann's alleged crimes were committed. Many argued that he could not get a fair trial in Israel, and should be tried in either an international tribunal or in a German court. After a lengthy trial, Eichmann was convicted and hanged. His body was cremated and his ashes scattered at sea so as not to sully Israeli soil.

After long negotiations, the West German government in 1953 recognized the participation of the German people in the murder of the Jews. The Federal Republic agreed to pay reparations to individual Jews, the Jewish people and the young state of Israel for the crimes of Nazi Germany. Payments were offered for confiscated property, material losses, wrongful incarceration, and slave labor. Nothing was offered for the dead.

Communist East Germany did not offer reparations. It regarded the Holocaust as a crime committed by Western capitalists. Only after Communist rule was ended did the East German Parliament apologize to the Jews. During its first session as a democratically elected body, the parliament admitted "joint responsibility on behalf of the people for the humiliation, expulsion and murder of Jewish women, men and children."

The history of the Holocaust cannot be closed quietly, shelved and forgotten with finality. For it is an ever present witness to our responsibility for each other and our growth as a moral and compassionate society.

*Thousands of forgotten shoes from Holocaust victims seem to echo the deceased bodies of their former owners. Any reusable item was taken from the Jews by their German captors. When Soviet troops entered Birkenau, they found 358,000 men's suits, 837,000 women's outfits and more than 15,400 pounds of women's hair packed into paper bags.*

*We are given our tomorrows*
*By those who gave us their todays . . .*